CIRCLE OF THE SEA

Creations from Oceania

Selections from the Oceania Collection

Museum of Natural History

Roger Williams Park Providence, Rhode Island

cover

MALE CROUCHING FIGURE

POLYNESIA, EASTER ISLAND, RAPA NUI

LATE 18TH- EARLY 19TH CENTURY   E3198

WOOD 20.64 X 6.98 CM

BROWN UNIVERSITY'S COLLEGE MUSEUM/JENKS MUSEUM

frontispiece and back flyleaf

SUPPORT FIGURE

POLYNESIA, HAWAIIAN ISLANDS

EARLY 19TH CENTURY   E2733

WOOD WITH DARK PIGMENT HIGHLIGHTS, EYES INLAID WITH SHELL

HEIGHT 39.4 CM

DONATED TO THE PROVIDENCE FRANKLIN SOCIETY BY

DANIEL TILLINGHAST ABORN BETWEEN 1829 AND 1831

ISBN 0-9646544-1-5

Printed in the USA

Copyright © 2002

Museum of Natural History

Providence Parks Department

Roger Williams Park

Providence, Rhode Island

TEXT AND ANALYSIS

Norman Hurst

Hurst Gallery

Cambridge, Massachusetts

ART DIRECTION AND DESIGN

Matter Inc.

North Kingstown, Rhode Island

PHOTOGRAPHY

Peter Bittner

Spring Street Digital, Inc.

Chappaqua, New York

Ira Garber

Providence, Rhode Island

(frontispiece)

COPYEDITING

Tracey Keough

Marilyn Massaro

PRINTING

Meridian Printing

East Greenwich, Rhode Island

TABLE OF CONTENTS

THE SMALL BUT RICH COLLECTION OF OBJECTS FEATURED IN THIS CATALOGUE AND THE exhibition it accompanies, were last seen by the public during the 1970s. The *Circle of the Sea* serves as a monument to the history of this late 19th century museum, to the spirit of adventure of the early collectors, and to the skill and innovation of the creators of these objects themselves.

Of the many people who contributed to the success of the project, a special thank you goes to Mayor Vincent A. Cianci, Jr. for his continuing support of the Museum. The inspiration for all we do comes from Superintendent of Parks, Nancy L. Derrig, who trusts in our abilities and allows us the freedom to be successful.

The expertly written text and analysis included in this publication are primarily the work of Norman Hurst, of Hurst Gallery in Cambridge, Massachusetts, a valued supporter and friend. The Museum's former Associate Curator, Jennifer Antes, worked closely with Norman, offering valuable insight. Katherine Burton Jones generously provided assistance with database development and Shana Dumont with copyediting.

The development of all aspects of the exhibition was the work of the Museum's own dedicated and talented staff. Many thanks to Marilyn Massaro, Judith Sweeney Lederman, Gary Holliday, Joanne Wilcox, Pasco Florio, Ronald Peck and Arnold Smith. Assistance with object conservation and inter- pretation was provided by A. Alexandra O'Donnell, Jere Barnard and Anne D'Alleva. The restoration of the exhibit gallery was facilitated by Robert McMahon, Deputy Superintendent of Parks and the architects at Durkee and Brown, Providence RI.

Many scholars, colleagues and friends provided assistance during a three-year NAGPRA dispute. Expert advice and generous support were offered by Dr. William H. Davenport, Rubellite Kawena Johnson, Herb Kawainui Kane, and Dr. Adrienne L. Kaeppler. Our attorney, Gregory L. Benik helped us navigate the review and litigation processes with his sound advice and sense of humor.

Finally, the exhibit was made possible through an exchange of gifts with Hui Mālama I Nā Kūpuna 'O Hawai'i Nei and the Office of Hawaiian Affairs. Our thanks to these organizations and their represen- tatives for help in, once again, making the Oceania collection available to the people of Rhode Island.

TRACEY KEOUGH, MUSEUM DIRECTOR

IN 1896 THE MUSEUM OF NATURAL HISTORY IN ROGER WILLIAMS PARK OPENED ITS
doors to a world on the brink of change. In just a few years, the horse-drawn carriages that transported its first visitors would give way to Model-Ts. The new electric lights that graced its halls were fitted out with gas jets as if to pay final tribute to a passing age. For the many dramatic changes the 20th century was to witness, the new Museum was poised and ready.

Designed in a richly ornate French Chateau style, the Museum was crafted as a monument to the sciences. It was indeed the regional response to what has been widely heralded as the "museum movement" of the late 19th and early 20th centuries. Often sited in city centers or in urban parks, museums were emblems of civic pride that embodied the hopes and aspirations of the communities that built them.

The Museum's founding was precipitated by a donation of 250 mounted birds and mammals to the City of Providence by former city resident John Steere of Santa Monica, California. It was built on the highest prospect in Roger Williams Park, designed in 1878 by landscape architect Horace William Shaler Cleveland. The Park itself is a classic example of the Urban Parks Movement that flowered in cities across America in the late 19th century. Today the 435 acre Park and its built environment are listed on the National Register of Historic Places.

From the original Steere donation the holdings of the fledgling Museum grew rapidly during its first two decades. By 1915, the need for additional exhibition space led to the construction of a new wing. Often called the "People's University," the Museum became a popular destination that offered an engaging place to visit and to learn amidst a city park campus.

Perhaps due to the expansion of exhibit space, the Museum became the beneficiary of a remarkable collection of artifacts from the "South Seas" in 1916. Among a list of eight "Special Ethnological Exhibits" in a museum pamphlet dated March 1, 1917, is "a collection of South Seas objects, tribute clubs and paddles, and war implements" from the Providence Franklin Society. The publication of this one page announcement of the Museum's cultural exhibits underscores the growing interest in and prominence of anthropology in natural history museums. Indeed, the roots of American anthropology as a discipline are found in the context of natural history museums.

Selections from the Museum's Oceania collection are reviewed in this catalogue which accompanies its namesake exhibition, *Circle of the Sea*. The artifacts featured were acquired from two primary sources, the Providence Franklin Society and the Jenks Museum at Brown University. These organizations and their history, relevant to the Museum's Oceania materials, have been described in "A Pacific Island Collection in Rhode Island," (1983). This report was generated by museum staff and scholars and was funded in part by a grant from the Rhode Island Committee for the Humanities. It represents what is, to date, the only formalized effort to link these objects with available archives. Researchers drew upon the records of the Providence Franklin Society, housed at the Rhode Island Historical Society in Providence. They also researched the Jenks Museum at the John Hay Library at Brown University. Accession records and archives housed in the Museum of Natural History were also consulted for the 1983 project and its report.

THE PACIFIC HALL, 1954.
FROM THE MUSEUM ARCHIVES.

It is therefore important to note a major conclusion of this report: its researchers stress the inadequate, incomplete and vague nature of many of the primary records at their disposal. For example, in the Providence Franklin Society's Records of Donations, many entries are listed as *lots*, e.g. "clubs and paddles" or "spears," making the task of associating these common artifact types with any specific Society donor virtually impossible. Since no catalogue or accession register for the "South Seas" objects accompanied the transfer, it is unknown whether all items listed in the Records of Donations were still present when transfer to the Museum occurred.

The Providence Franklin Society was a local philosophical organization comprised of members from the privileged class who convened weekly for lectures and who maintained a collection or "cabinet." Commencing with the gathering of a few associates in 1820 who met in each others' homes, the Society first called itself the Providence Philosophical Association. It held its first formal meeting under this name in April, 1822, when a slate of officers was chosen for the ensuing year. In October that year, the Association changed its name to the Providence Franklin Society.

The Society continued to meet regularly, hold public lectures, maintain collections, and publish scholarly materials over a century-long history. Its members came from all walks of life including merchants, sea captains and shipmasters, scholars, physicians and amateur naturalists. An 1829 pamphlet published by the Society gave detailed instructions for collecting and preserving natural history specimens. It also encouraged the gathering of cultural materials that might illustrate "...the manners and customs of other people." That this inspired members to amass cultural "curiosities" for their Cabinet is documented by the many objects attributable to the Society in this catalogue.

By 1912, faced with a declining membership and the inability to adequately showcase its collections, the Society began to seek other repositories for its holdings. Harold L. Madison, Museum Director, made a strong case for the South Seas material coming to Roger Williams Park. Plans were already underway for the construction of a new wing at the Museum. Exhibited there, the collection would be publicly accessible to hundreds of people, a goal never realized by the Society.

Upon completion of the new wing, in 1916 the South Seas component of the Providence Franklin Society's collection was transferred to the Museum under Madison's direction. The Society voted to disband in January 1922, a motion that carried by a single vote among a mere eleven members.

The second major source of the Museum's Oceania material is Brown University's Jenks Museum, which closed c. 1930. In 1891, this campus museum was named for John Whipple Potter Jenks (1819-1894), Professor of Zoology at Brown. Jenks served as the museum's curator and was its most ardent advocate.

Upon his death, having lost its principle advocate, and coupled with the University's growing need for space, the museum languished and ultimately closed. In 1931, nine artifacts were donated to the Museum of Natural History from Brown and its former Jenks Museum; seven of these were of Pacific Island origin. Once again, in 1954, still more Oceanic objects from the Jenks Museum were located at Brown and offered to the Museum, adding another seventy artifacts to the assemblage. No catalogue records or any other kind of documentation accompanied the transfer of the Jenks material.

This new donation coincided with the creation of an exhibit of the material from Oceania. Many of these new acquisitions were included in the Museum's new Pacific Hall. Its development was the work of Museum Director, Maribelle Cormack, who kept a detailed journal documenting her accomplishments, including lists and locations of objects on exhibit, interpretive labels, press clippings, photographs and personal observations. Photographs interspersed throughout Cormack's journal depict the arrangement of objects in their cases, highlighting some of the most "important" items in the collection. Among these were three figures from Easter Island, a spear rest from Hawaii, a Marquesas Islands post figure, a tattooed head from New Zealand and a stick god figure from Hawaii.

CONSTRUCTION OF THE MUSEUMS'S NORTH WING NEARS COMPLETION IN JULY 1915. FROM THE MUSEUM ARCHIVES.

The Pacific Hall opened on May 11, 1954. Of the night's festivities Cormack wrote, "That was a night. I do not recall an occasion just like it. The gods of the Pacific shed their light upon us...The Museum held a new spirit of adventure." Indeed the opening of the Pacific Hall, coupled with that of the Planetarium the year before, helped to revitalize an institution that had lost much of its luster in the years following World War II.

The Pacific Hall was de-installed in the late 1970s. The objects were returned to storage and the gallery became home to a number of short term ethnographic exhibits. By the mid-1980s it was completely closed to the public, becoming a storage area for a variety of other collections. Sadly, lack of climate control, coupled with persistent leaking from the ductwork above the ceiling, marred the beauty of the Museum's only remaining original gallery. Its architectural integrity and the condition of its cabinets and fixtures began to decay rapidly. Hidden beneath a haze of plastic drop cloths, the vintage mahogany and glass casework was in dire need of restoration. Over the course of a century the woodwork was badly scratched; brass handrails on floor cases were broken and missing trim; the oak floors had been covered by a layer of linoleum tiles. Overhead, an expanse of skylights had been painted over. Cracked and fallen plaster from walls and ceiling were further reminders of lost Victorian splendor.

Like the former Pacific Hall itself, the Oceania collection also languished for many years. The 1983 report was an attempt to renew scholarly interest in the small but rich collection while providing the basis for a new exhibition of the Pacific Island material. There was an ongoing interest in showcasing the collection from Oceania in order to highlight the rich and wonderful legacy of material obtained by whalers, merchants and sea captains who traveled to this region from New England's shores.

The entire collection was much in need of conservation and many objects required extensive repair; the gallery was not suitable for use as an exhibition space in its dilapidated state. The Museum itself was suffering from demographic changes in the city's neighborhoods, a shortage of adequate staff and declining visitor numbers. In the late 1980s and early 1990s several attempts were made to secure funds for the full scale conservation and exhibition of the collection, but without success.

The Oceania collection suffered not only from benign neglect but from the theft of one significant piece and the attempted theft of another. In 1976, the Museum loaned an item described in accession records as a "carved wood post figure (stick god figure) from Hawaii" to the Whitney Museum of American Art for its exhibition, *Two Hundred Years of American Sculpture*. The object was stolen from the Whitney two months after the exhibition opened. It was never recovered. A decade later another significant object, a spear rest (or support figure) from Hawaii, was stolen from the safe deposit box in which it was stored. The figure (see frontispiece and back flyleaf) was recovered soon afterward but administrators were aware that this exceedingly rare object was at continued risk due to the inadequate security and storage conditions.

At that time, the Museum administration was contacted by representatives from Sotheby's with an offer to include the support figure in its trial art auction in the fall of 1986. The rarity (and resulting high appraisal value) of the support figure made it an unlikely candidate for exhibition at the Museum which, at the time, did not have the resources for exhibit development, nor the means to properly secure the Hawaiian figure. The administration viewed this as an opportunity to obtain the funding needed for the long-awaited conservation, analysis and exhibition of the Pacific Islands material. The sale of the spear rest was approved by the Board of Park Commissioners, in accordance with the rules governing the disposition of property belonging to the City of Providence.

On November 18, 1986, the "Hawaiian Islands Support Figure" was included among the items in Sotheby's *Important Tribal Art* auction in New York. To the surprise of all concerned, and in spite of its having been featured on the cover of the auction catalogue, the piece did not sell. Still without adequate security or plans for its exhibition, it was decided to leave the figure in secure storage at Sotheby's, where it remained for ten years.

The early 1990's saw some remarkable renovations at the Museum, including: a new roof; the restoration of the lobby and central staircase; the creation of climate-controlled, customized storage; and installation of a building-wide HVAC system. In 1994, an overhaul of Museum exhibits and programs began. The revitalization plan included: the development of a hands-on, discovery-based menu of education programs for schools, the creation of comprehensive professional development opportunities for teachers, the renovation of the classroom/auditorium, the re-opening of the Planetarium, the development of an exhibit highlighting the Native American collection, and the publication of its first exhibition catalogue. Unfortunately, this plan did not allow for the extensive

THE OLD PACIFIC HALL PRIOR TO
RENOVATION IN 1999.
FROM THE MUSEUM ARCHIVES.

CIRCLE OF THE SEA EXHIBITION
IN THE RENOVATED GALLERY, 2002.
FROM THE MUSEUM ARCHIVES.

renovation of the old Pacific Hall that would be necessary to re-open it: nor did it permit the conservation, analysis and exhibition of the Oceania collection.

In December, 1995, the Museum received an inquiry from an individual who had attended the 1986 Sotheby's auction and was still suffering "buyer's remorse" at not having bid on the Hawaiian support figure at that time. The administration was once again faced with a difficult decision regarding the de-accessioning and sale of an object in the collection. Once again, it recognized a unique opportunity to secure the funding necessary to allow for the complete conservation, analysis and exhibition of the Oceania collection.

With permission from the Board of Park Commissioners, the Museum staff pursued the possibility of the sale. In the three years that followed, the Hawaiian support figure would become the focus of a lengthy dispute under the Native American Graves Protection and Repatriation Act (NAGPRA) of 1990.

Following a newspaper report that prematurely announced its pending sale, the Museum was contacted by representatives of the Native Hawaiian organizations, Hui Mālama I Nā Kūpuna 'O Hawai'i Nei and the Office of Hawaiian Affairs regarding the status of the support figure with regard to NAGPRA. It was decided to suspend any plans to sell the support figure until a thorough review could be conducted and further consultation between the parties could take place.

The position taken by Hui Mālama and the Office of Hawaiian Affairs was that, based on oral traditions, the object was a god figure and therefore "sacred" as defined in NAGPRA. Further, they believed that the "sacred" status of the object would not have allowed for its alienation by any member of the social group.

STICK GOD FIGURE FROM HAWAII (REPLICA). FROM THE MUSEUM ARCHIVES.

As Museum records relative to the Oceania collection are vague, references concerning the category of Hawaiian sculpture classified as support figures were consulted. Anthropological literary sources indicated that these ornamental spear rests were owned by individuals of rank and were strictly utilitarian in nature, being lashed to a canoe to hold spears or poles for fishing. Facts gleaned from these references were reinforced through our consultations with highly respected scholars and experts in Hawaiian culture, art and language.

Consultation, as required by NAGPRA, between the Museum and the Native Hawaiian organizations did not result in a resolution; the matter was then referred to the NAGPRA Review Committee for consideration in November, 1996. The Committee's initial finding was that the object was "sacred" as defined in NAGPRA. Further, they accepted the assertion that such status would not have allowed for its alienation by the original owner and therefore the Museum would not have "right of possession."

Following the November ruling, the City of Providence initiated a lawsuit in federal district court challenging certain provisions of NAGPRA on constitutional grounds. All parties were subsequently advised that the Review Committee would withhold its formal advisory finding, pending the presentation of further evidence at its next hearing.

Representatives of both groups appeared before the Review Committee for a second time in March, 1997; the Museum presented testimony from four individuals (both Native and non-Native Hawaiians) who are recognized experts in Hawaiian culture, art and language. Once again the committee addressed three issues: whether the object constituted a "sacred object" under NAGPRA; whether either side presented sufficient evidence with regard to "right of possession"; and whether the City of Providence should repatriate the object to the Native Hawaiian organizations.

The committee first concluded that the support figure was a "sacred object." The basis for this finding was unclear. The Review Committee simply deferred to the representations of the Native Hawaiian organizations, disregarding the presentations given by experts on behalf of the Museum.

With respect to "right of possession," the committee concluded that, based upon the evidence, it could not make any determination. In the absence of a finding that the Native Hawaiian organizations demonstrated that the City of Providence did not have "right of possession" under NAGPRA, the City continued to "own" the object.

In February, 1998, after a two year dispute, litigation and court-ordered mediation, an agreement was reached between Hui Mālama, the Office of Hawaiian Affairs and the City of Providence. The agreement was based on mutual respect and interest in serving the people of Providence and Native Hawaiians, and consisted of an exchange of gifts between the parties. The Museum's gift was the return of the support figure to the Native Hawaiian organizations. Their gift to the Museum was in the form of a donation to fund the conservation, analysis and exhibition of the Oceania collection along with the renovation of the old Pacific Hall. The formal exchange of gifts took place on the steps of the Museum in August, 1998.

After more than two decades, the Oceania collection would finally be accessible to the public again. Many Museum visitors remembered the old Pacific Hall and had asked to see this material again. The renovation of the Museum's only original gallery would offer a premier exhibition space for the collection while offering visitors a glimpse of past Victorian elegance.

In June, 2000, the *Circle of the Sea* exhibition opened in the newly restored Pacific Hall after a two-year renovation. During these same two years, the Oceania collection itself underwent complete conservation and repair. Each object in the collection was meticulously cleaned, reviewed and appraised. The creation of a collection database facilitated documentation and record-keeping in preparation for the exhibit and its companion catalogue.

In 1912, the Providence Franklin Society was persuaded to transfer the Pacific islands material to the Museum on the promise that it would be seen by hundreds of people. Now, in the *Circle of the Sea* exhibit and catalogue, the collection is accessible to tens of thousand of people each year.

The Museum collects natural history specimens and cultural artifacts assembled, primarily by local collectors, from sites around the world. We care for and conserve what has been entrusted to us, and use it to teach and inspire the public. We continue to search for innovative ways to fill our role as the "People's University," helping children and families learn about the wonders of our world and its people. For the many dramatic changes the 21st century will witness, the Museum remains poised and ready.

TRACEY KEOUGH, MUSEUM DIRECTOR

MARILYN MASSARO, CURATOR OF COLLECTIONS

SUPPORT FIGURE
POLYNESIA, HAWAIIAN ISLANDS
EARLY 19TH CENTURY
FROM THE MUSEUM ARCHIVES.

THE FOLLOWING EXPLAIN THE TERMS THAT ACCOMPANY THE OBJECTS.

Catalogue Number
The number assigned to objects as they appear in the catalogue

Object name
The common Anglo-European name for the object

Native name (italicized)
The common native name for the object, if known

Geo-cultural Region, Island or Island chain
The geo-cultural designations of Polynesia, Micronesia and Melanesia are used for general location, followed by attribution to a specific island or island chain within those regions

Approximate date of manufacture
The time period when the object was most likely to have been manufactured, plus or minus twenty-five years

Museum catalogue number
The multiple digit number (preceded by "E") assigned to the object by the museum

Materials of construction
The materials, such as wood, plant fiber, shell, pigment, etc., used to make the objects

Measurements
Dimensions were taken from the longest and the widest points on the object

Source of object
The name of the collector, donor or place of exchange

Description
The anthropological and aesthetic interpretive analysis of the object

SCULPTURE AND IMAGE

ALTHOUGH FIGURAL SCULPTURE IS PRODUCED THROUGHOUT THE PACIFIC ISLANDS, ITS frequency and significance varies considerably among Melanesian, Polynesian, and Micronesian cultures. Sculpture is relatively common in Melanesian cultures in both secular and religious contexts. Clan or totemic animals and other imagery are numerous, as are images representative of ancestors. Images may be found on the most mundane implements, such as digging sticks, as well as within the sacred confines of secret societies' meeting places.

The betel nut pestle, Catalogue No. 8, is a Melanesian "secular" object decorated with figural sculpture. The canoe charm, Catalogue No. 10 is a sculpture made for a spiritual purpose. Sometimes these distinctions can be moot, however, as when a utilitarian object becomes sacred from its association with an important event or individual.

In Polynesian and Micronesian cultures images occur with far less frequency. Polynesian and Micronesian cultures have closely related sculptural forms and functions. Although there are no examples of Micronesian sculpture in the Museum of Natural History's collection there are several examples of Polynesian figural representation.

Sculpture in Polynesia, usually representing deities or deified ancestors, tended to be in the possession or under the control of members of the privileged *ali'i* class. In addition, images on secular objects like the Maori treasure box Catalogue No. 35, the Marquesan stilt step Catalogue No. 37, and the Tongan club Catalogue No. 65, served to emphasize their owner's hierarchical or divine origins. Thus Polynesian images reinforced the hereditary entitlement of their owners, who traced their lineages back to deified ancestors and ultimately to the gods.

CATALOGUE NO. 1
ARCHITECTURAL SUPPORT FIGURE
POLYNESIA, MARQUESAS ISLANDS
PROBABLY EARLY TO MID-19TH CENTURY

In Melanesian society on the other hand, "Big Men" achieved status by personal initiative and the support of family, friends, and neighbors. The practice of commissioning images and sculpture was a part of the system of personal striving and social elevation reflective of an individual's growing importance and status in his community. In many Melanesian cultural contexts women also underwent parallel processes of social advancement. However, these women's rites were not characteristically marked by the ceremonial production of images and sculpture.

In Melanesian society, the most powerful and significant sculpture would be associated with important living individuals or with their immediate ancestors. Generally, age diminished the power of an object and the most significant art was that associated with or created by the most important people or forces of the "here and now." In Polynesian society, by contrast, the most powerful and significant sculpture would be that which validated the lineage of the ruling high born individuals; such images might have been created many generations in the past.

The stone megaliths of Easter Island are perhaps the most familiar expression of Polynesian public sculpture. On sacred platforms, *morai*, the high born of specific *moieties*, or kinship groups, could worship and commune with their deified ancestors who were specifically summoned to inhabit the images that had been erected there. The assertion of this connection backward through generations to these ancestral deities was paramount in Polynesian religious practice, especially among the *ali'i* in eastern Polynesia.

The realistic depiction of individuals, animals, or plants is not characteristic of most Pacific island art styles. Indeed the similarity of one statue to another is a distinct characteristic of both Melanesian and Polynesian statuary. Sculpture tends more to incorporate design elements that may be associated with clan animals or other specific imagery evocative of a cultural mythos.

In Melanesian societies, virtually every member of a village would have his or her clan or totemic references. Any individual thus associated with a particular clan might properly use such imagery on canoes, bowls, textiles, personal accessories, or weapons. "Big Men" might have larger or more impressive personal accessories, however all individuals related or associated in a Melanesian clan or moiety might have houses or personal property decorated with appropriate imagery.

By contrast, as previously noted, Polynesian use of figurative forms was limited to elevated individuals. Misappropriation by commoners would have been in violation of strict *taboo* and would have been dangerous if not fatal. The relative scarcity of sculpture and imagery in Polynesian society is also due to the amount of time that has elapsed since these societies gave up their indigenous religious and cultural mores.

Many of the most sacred images from some Polynesian cultures were constructed of relatively fragile materials, including barkcloth, wicker, basketry, and other fibers. They were frequently elaborated with fugitive pigments, brightly colored feathers, and applications of ephemeral plant material. Most of the Polynesian religious images from the early contact period have been lost. Many were deliberately destroyed by foreign missionaries or native converts.

detail
CATALOGUE NO. 1

This was the case in Tahiti and the Society Islands which underwent large-scale conversions early in the 19th century. Parallel developments also affected cultural continuity in the Hawaiian Islands where King Kamehameha II (Liholiho) abolished the Hawaiian *kapu* and religious system in 1819. Religious images were ordered to be destroyed. All these events predated the founding of the Providence Franklin Society, in 1822, whose collection is the largest single component of the Museum's current Pacific island holdings.

Accordingly, societies that retained their indigenous cultures into the mid-19th century are more fully represented in the collection by sculptures and objects with figurative imagery. Notably these areas include New Zealand, Easter Island, the Marquesas Islands and the cultural complex comprising Tonga and Fiji. Almost every Polynesian culture had discontinued the production of images for traditional use over a century ago. Some cultures in Melanesia, by contrast, have continued to produce and use sculpture for spiritual and traditional social purposes, even into the 21st century.

The Polynesian images in the Museum's collection are few, reflective of the paucity of surviving Polynesian sculpture worldwide. For a relatively small collection, however, there are a surprising number of noteworthy figurative objects.

In addition to the Hawaiian support figure, the frontispiece, there are three early figures from Easter Island, Catalogue Nos. 2, 3, and 4. The cultural significance of the Easter Island figures is not well understood. However, it is certain that they constituted heirloom property worn or proudly displayed by their owners on important ceremonial occasions.

The production of images or "idols" declined rapidly with the introduction of Christianity. Many objects were destroyed by the zeal of missionaries and their native converts. Some religious images reached Western collections because they were released as an alternative to this deliberate destruction.

Some island populations were the victims of imported diseases and of "black-birding" foreigners who kidnapped indigenous peoples for slave labor. Sculptures may have been acquired from abandoned caches, disused structures, disinterested heirs, or appropriated by native traders from defunct lineages as a consequence of this widespread depopulation.

counter-clockwise from top left

CATALOGUE NO. 2
LIZARD FIGURE *MOKO*
POLYNESIA, EASTER ISLAND, *RAPA NUI*
LATE 18TH- EARLY 19TH CENTURY

CATALOGUE NO. 3
MALE CROUCHING FIGURE
POLYNESIA, EASTER ISLAND, *RAPA NUI*
LATE 18TH- EARLY 19TH CENTURY

CATALOGUE NO. 4
MALE FIGURE *MOAI KAVAKAVA*
POLYNESIA, EASTER ISLAND, *RAPA NUI*
EARLY 19TH CENTURY

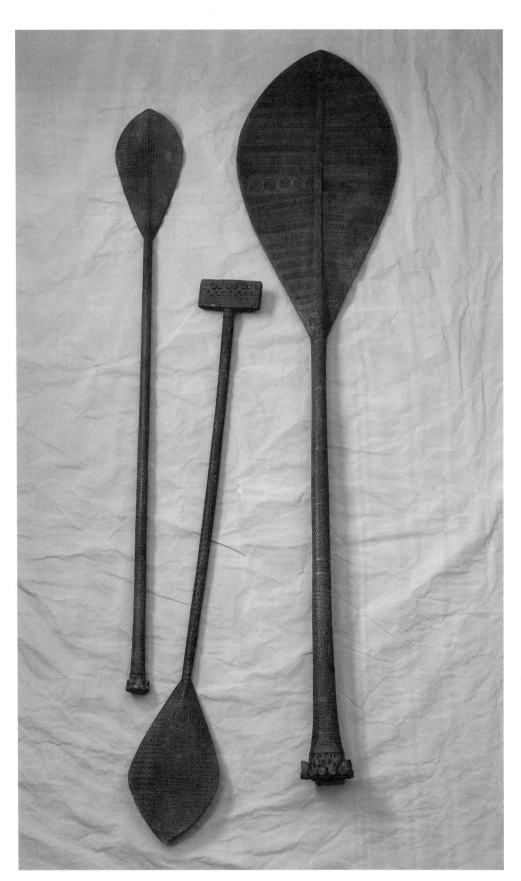

detail
CATALOGUE NO. 7

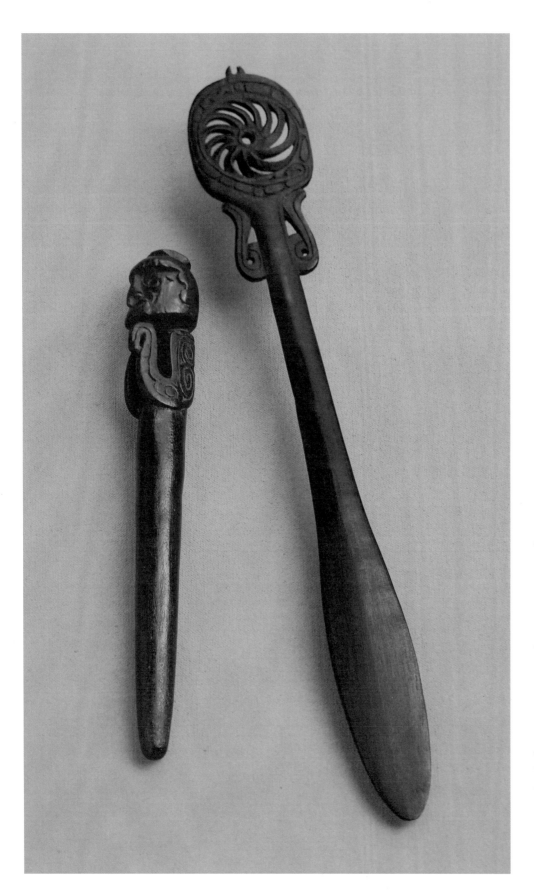

CATALOGUE NO. 8
BETEL NUT PESTLE
MELANESIA, PAPUA NEW GUINEA,
MILNE BAY PROVINCE, MASSIM
EARLY 20TH CENTURY

CATALOGUE NO. 9
LIME SPATULA
MELANESIA, PAPUA NEW GUINEA,
MILNE BAY PROVINCE, LOUISIADE ARCHIPELAGO
PROBABLY EARLY 20TH CENTURY

facing page
CATALOGUE NO. 10
CANOE PROW FIGURE *TOTOISHU* OR *MUSU MUSU*
MELANESIA, SOLOMON ISLANDS
19TH CENTURY

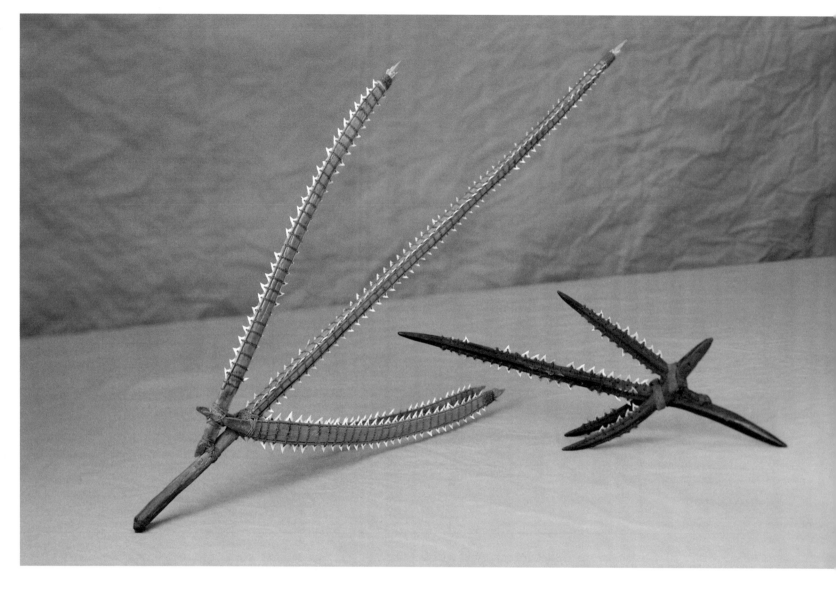

from left to right

CATALOGUE NO. 11

WEAPON *RERE* OR *BETIA*

MICRONESIA, KIRIBATI

PROBABLY LATE 19TH CENTURY

CATALOGUE NO. 12

WEAPON *RERE* OR *BETIA*

MICRONESIA, KIRIBATI

19TH CENTURY

detail

CATALOGUE NO. 12

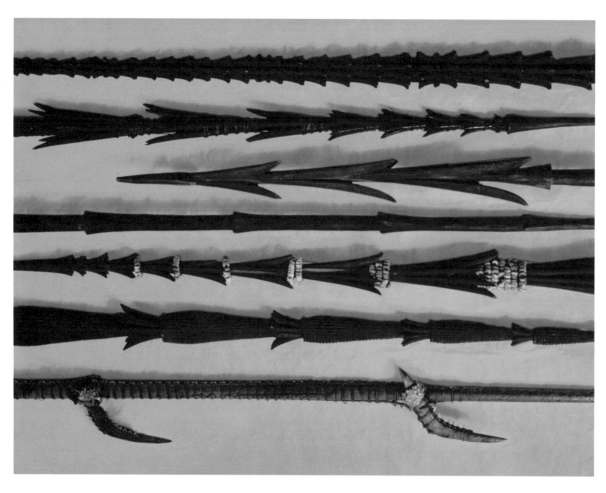

CATALOGUE NO. 16
SPEAR *MOTO*
POLYNESIA, FIJI
PROBABLY EARLY 19TH CENTURY

CATALOGUE NO. 17
SPEAR *GADREGADRE*
POLYNESIA, FIJI
19TH CENTURY

CATALOGUE NO. 18
SPEAR *TIKAU*
POLYNESIA, FIJI
19TH CENTURY

CATALOGUE NO. 19
WEAPON *RERE* OR *BETIA*
MICRONESIA, KIRIBATI
19TH CENTURY

from top to bottom
CATALOGUE NO. 13
SPEAR *SOKILAKI-VAI*
POLYNESIA, FIJI
19TH CENTURY

CATALOGUE NO. 14
SPEAR *TIKAU*
POLYNESIA, FIJI
EARLY 19TH CENTURY

CATALOGUE NO. 15
SPEAR *GADREGADRE*
POLYNESIA, FIJI
EARLY 19TH CENTURY

WEAPONS AND WARFARE

AS REPORTED BY EARLY VISITORS TO THE PACIFIC, ARMED CONFLICTS AND HOSTILITIES were commonplace intra- and inter-island occurrences. Small raids by neighboring groups might injure or kill as few as a single victim, but could subsequently spiral into huge conflicts affecting generations in cycles of revenge killings. The histories of both New Zealand and Fiji are marked by nearly a century of bloody violence, only diminishing by the end of the 1860s and 70s respectively.

The use of traditional clubs, especially for hand to hand combat persisted after contact, but firearms provided an advantage that allowed certain groups to gain the upper hand in overwhelming shows of force and ultimate slaughter. Throughout the 19th century in New Zealand, firearms were in great supply, culminating in the "Maori Wars" of the 1860s.

The extent to which the Maori had learned "the European art of War" was demonstrated at the battle of Nukumaru, January 25th, 1865. Six hundred Maori, including equestrians, matched their firepower and field tactics "in broad daylight" against 963 British troops, who included artillery, cavalry, and two regiments of the Royal Engineers. The British only succeeded in winning, according to Alexander, by reason of "steady discipline...and the excellence of their arms" (1873:244-5).

Both Maori and Fijian combatants relied on clubs like those presented here for fighting in close quarters. The *taiaha* of the Maori was a status symbol, prestige staff, and weapon all in one. Fijians carried a variety of two-handed clubs at most times, however, the *ula* or throwing club was especially ubiquitous. A Fijian man might wear two or more *ula* thrust through his loincloth or *malo*.

There is a complex mixing of cultures in the Fiji Islands, which were a magnet for fortune-seeking warriors from Tonga and Samoa. Some eventually settled on land awarded as war spoils by victorious Fijian chiefs. The Fijians esteemed the Tongans as canoe builders, ivory workers, and exceptional sailors. Many artifacts collected in Fiji were imported or created in Fiji by Samoan or Tongan mercenaries.

In the Eastern Solomon Islands, from which several of the weapons in the collection originate, inter-island raids were documented as recently as the late 19th century. Solomon Islanders were not especially good open ocean sailors, however they constructed large canoes that were capable of transporting dozens of warriors to invasion sites. Some of these same vessels brought native inhabitants out to greet European visitors. Bellicose receptions were repeatedly reported by European and American sailors.

The earliest of these, Alvaro de Mendaña in 1568, recounted virtually interminable attacks from canoes loaded with warriors in the Solomon Islands. One of the artists on Captain James Cook's voyages in the 1770s records a war canoe filled with Maori, gesturing defiantly and brandishing weapons as a greeting to his crew. As late as 1841, the United States Exploring (Wilkes) Expedition visited the Fiji Islands specifically to redress violent receptions the peoples there had accorded American visitors.

In Melanesia, combat weapons manufacture has continued to modern times. In more remote parts of the island of New Guinea, bows and arrows, shields, spears and spear-throwers are still employed in tribal warfare; however, modern firearms have also been in use in these areas for decades.

The variety of technology, forms, and styles of elaboration of the weapons originating among pre-European contact Pacific Island peoples is truly astonishing. Rock projectiles thrown and slung are among the simplest of these. Elaborately carved clubs decorated with figures and embellished with ivory inlay are some of the most intricate and beautiful.

Naturally, sailors and other foreign male visitors to the Pacific traded goods for weapons, as many native men would have carried little more than their weapons in initial encounters with visitors. This trade process "liberated" many of the early contact weapons in surprisingly large numbers. In the early post-contact period, a few nails, a jackknife, or a worn file might have been considered ample compensation for an armload of wooden clubs, laboriously carved by stone-age technology. Pacification of many of the island groups, especially Polynesian ones, led to the cessation of production of most weapons by the middle to late 19th century. Thereafter, a few weapons became available as obsolete relics of a former time.

The Museum of Natural History's collection is especially rich in weapons. The most numerous examples come from the Fiji Islands in western Polynesia and Kiribati in the Micronesian area. Most of these date to the first half of the 19th century; whalers were frequent visitors to both areas during this period.

Polynesian peoples fashioned clubs and spears, and their fighting traditions favored hand to hand combat. Aside from its use in Fiji, where Melanesian strains are in evidence, the bow and arrow was unknown as a weapon. Neither were shields employed in Polynesian fighting traditions. The Polynesian arsenal nonetheless consisted of a bewildering variety of forms and decorative styles of short clubs, long clubs, pole clubs, spears, and projectile weapons.

Large bone-crushing maces and other clubs from Fiji, thin spatulate hand clubs from the Maori of New Zealand, and mid-length clubs from Samoa and Tonga with finely carved surface details, are just a few of the more common examples which appear in collections worldwide. Elaborately barbed spears, some over ten feet in length, were especially daunting. The long, heavy, paddle shaped weapon, *pa'ahua*, of the Marquesas Islands, was wielded in horizontal sweeping motions with devastating results.

Although designed as lethal weapons, these implements are also beautiful examples of the art and design of their creators. Elegant abstract shapes, fine engraved designs, dramatically contoured striking sections, and carefully crafted, sometimes ivory- or bone-inlaid butts and shafts, are all found in the corpus of Polynesian weaponry. Many of the decorative motifs appear to imitate basketry or fiber; others suggest designs found in body ornament or decorated barkcloth.

Some weapon shapes have been likened to naturally occurring forms, like the Samoan coconut stalk club, *uatongi* and the lotus club or *gu-gu* of Fiji, which may have been intended to represent a plant or, alternatively, a species of fish. Among the imposing arsenal of Fijian clubs, the smallest club, *ula*, was the most feared because it could be thrown with deadly accuracy over a considerable distance.

In contrast to the Polynesian weapons, almost entirely fashioned from dense, hard, woods, the weapons of Micronesian Kiribati, which also abound in the collection, are made of palm wood lashed with numerous rows of shark teeth, secured by coconut fiber and human hair. Human hair was also woven into coconut fiber armor in geometric patterns.

The range in variety, lengths, and forms of these shark tooth-edged weapons is remarkable. From small daggers, probably for use by women, to lances up to three meters in length, some sport forked members, others terminate in clusters of stingray barbs. Accounts of early visitors are replete with incidents documenting the employment of all these types.

Armed conflicts using these traditional weapons usually resulted in the strongest or most able fighter emerging victorious. The increasing widespread use of firearms however, introduced a random quality to the fatalities and changed the tenor of conflicts especially in the 19th century. Because a powerful chief or a fleeing coward might be killed with equal ease, warfare ceased to have the personal validating connotation that it had in the days before munitions were readily available. Even many Fijian war canoes were equipped with cannon during the post-contact period. As a reaction, heavy fortifications and trenches were laboriously constructed around towns or to secure strategic locations and could be proof against the firepower of even heavy artillery.

detail
CATALOGUE NO. 49

clockwise from top left

CATALOGUE NO. 20
COVERED BOWL WITH SHELL INLAY
MICRONESIA, PALAU
PROBABLY LATE 19TH CENTURY

CATALOGUE NO. 21
COVERED BOWL WITH SHELL INLAY
MICRONESIA, PALAU
LATE 19TH- EARLY 20TH CENTURY

CATALOGUE NO. 22
PLATTER *ONPAL* OR *ONGALL*
MICRONESIA, PALAU
LATE 19TH- EARLY 20TH CENTURY

CATALOGUE NO. 23
NECKLACE
MICRONESIA, MARSHALL ISLANDS
PROBABLY 20TH CENTURY

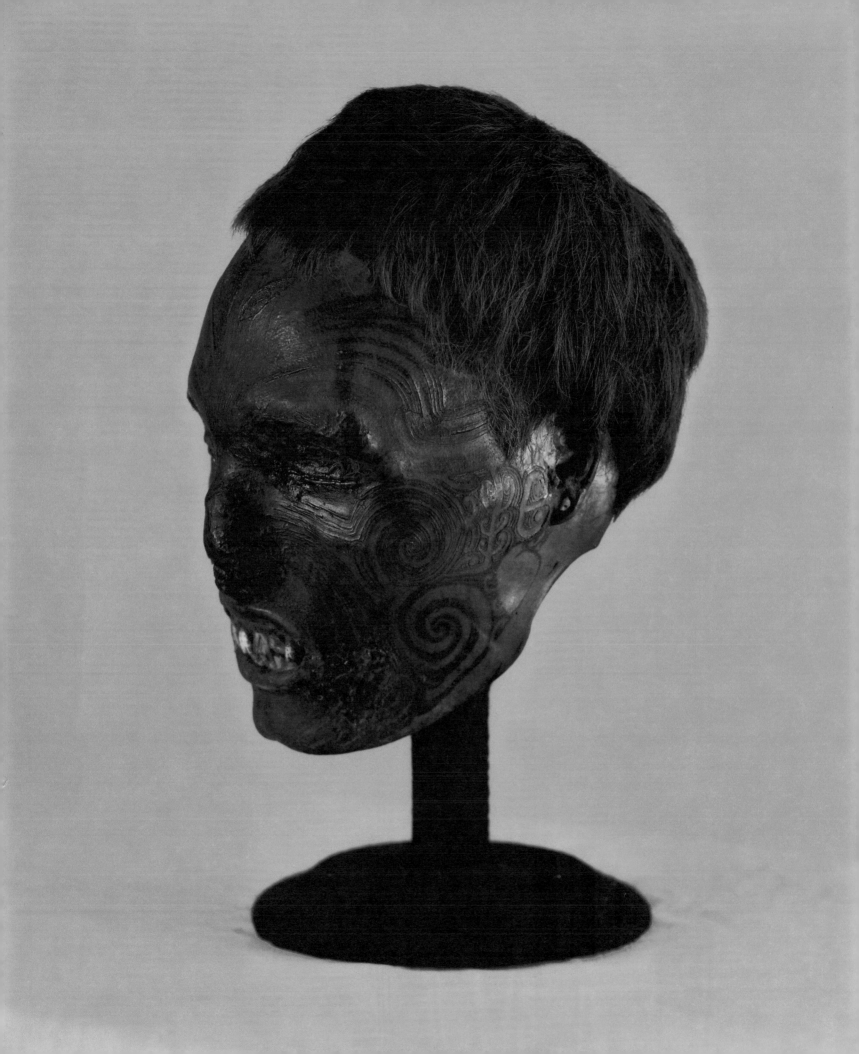

TATTOO AND ORNAMENT

BODY ORNAMENT VARIED AMONG THE PEOPLES OF THE PACIFIC ISLANDS ACCORDING TO culture and available materials. Beads and other pendants used in necklaces, belts, and body ornament were made of nut, wood, shell, tooth, and stone on plant fiber or human hair strands. The most common of these fibers was braided coconut fiber. The wearing of pins, combs, or other decoration in the hair, ear ornaments, and arm or leg ornaments in the form of shell bracelets, woven bands, or composite creations was widespread.

Rare shells or feathers might make an ornament especially precious. Certain materials for the manufacture of prestige ornaments were obtained in trade. Turtle or seashell might be obtained from shore dwellers; feathers and quarried stone typically came from upland sources.

Some body ornament was created for specific use on important ceremonial occasions. Hereditary status, gender, and age were determining factors in specific body decoration. An individual's elevation in rank, a wedding, or the funeral of an important person might be observed in part by the wearing of special cosmetic applications, ornaments, or costumes.

Some special ornaments constituted family heirloom treasure, especially among Polynesian cultures. They passed from generation to generation, accumulating personal power or *mana* with each successive owner. The Maori treasure box, *wakahuia*, Catalogue No. 35, is itself an heirloom that would have contained such valued ornaments and personal accessories.

Perhaps the most important ornament in the collection is the Hawaiian sperm whale tooth necklace, *lei niho palaoa*, Catalogue No. 25. Composed of multiple strands of finely square-braided human hair and a much-worn and polished sperm whale ivory pendant, this object is a remarkable example of chiefly Polynesian ornament. It was undoubtedly used for generations before it found its way into the collection. Not only was the ivory pendant of great prestige value, but the actual hair, having come from highborn female relatives, would have constituted material of great *mana* or potency to its entitled male or female possessor.

In addition to wearable ornament, Pacific peoples, especially Polynesian and Micronesian, practiced tattoo. Among Melanesian peoples, body piercing and scarification was practiced widely. Ears, nose, lips, and genitalia were frequent loci for tattoo, perforation, modification, or surgery.

CATALOGUE NO. 24
TATTOOED HEAD *MOKOMOKAI*
POLYNESIA, NEW ZEALAND, MAORI
EARLY 19TH CENTURY

Among the Washkuk in Papua New Guinea, young men still undergo torso scarification, which produces raised welts. The resultant patterns imitate the hide of the crocodile, the most powerful and aggressive animal of the area. Initiates are scarified and exhorted to emulate the attributes of the crocodile themselves.

Ornaments of shell, bone, tusk, or other more ephemeral materials might be inserted through the nasal septum, ear lobes, or other bodily perforations. Plumes or pins might be worn according to the preference of the wearer.

Polynesian and Micronesian peoples designed and wore full body tattoo often of spectacular intricacy and beauty. To have extensive tattoo was the prerogative only of individuals of hereditary chiefly rank. Undergoing this tattoo process was expensive, dangerous, and circumscribed by many restrictions or taboos. The individual being tattooed might have multiple sessions over the course of many years to achieve the complete design. Men's tattoo was usually more extensive than that of women, but this varied from culture to culture. Designs were produced using needles or comb-like perforating instruments that were soaked with pigment and tapped through the surface of the skin using a delicate tattooing hammer. The collection has examples of both these tools.

The Maori of New Zealand were unique among Polynesians in actually carving the skin surface away in minute grooves with a sharp tattooing chisel. Dark pigment was then applied in the grooves where it would be absorbed, making the scarring more visible when it healed. This special form of Maori tattoo, *moko*, reflects Maori decorative art style consisting of elaborate spiral designs comprising specific, though abstract, images.

The Maori are also believed to be unique in their tradition of preserving the heads of their venerated deceased by a process of drying and smoking them over the fire. Such preserved heads, *mokomokai*, constituted treasured heirloom property in their own right and were uncovered and displayed on important occasions as part of family rites and remembrances. After contact with foreigners in the late 18th century, the Maori began beheading and preserving the tattooed heads of their enemies as spoils of war and for subsequent trade. The collection includes a *mokomokai*, Catalogue No. 24, whose designs are still quite clear.

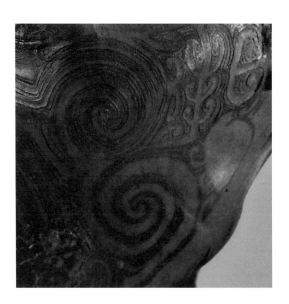

detail
CATALOGUE NO. 24

facing page
CATALOGUE NO. 25
NECKLACE *LEI NIHO PALAOA*
POLYNESIA, HAWAIIAN ISLANDS
EARLY 19TH CENTURY

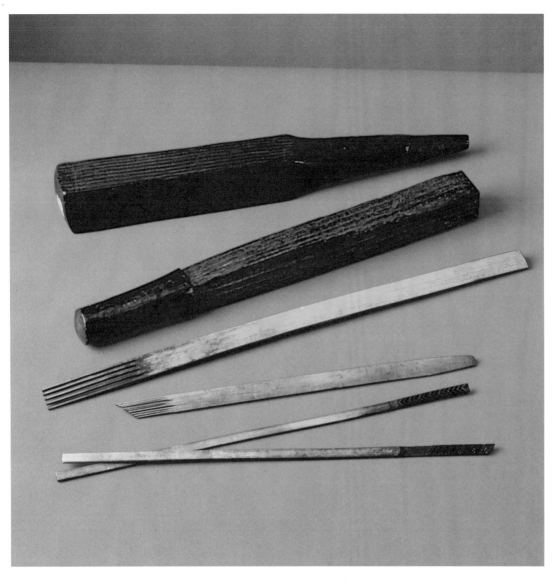

from top to bottom
CATALOGUE NO. 26
BARCLOTH SECOND STAGE BEATER *I'E KUKU*
POLYNESIA, HAWAIIAN ISLANDS
19TH CENTURY

CATALOGUE NO. 27
BARCLOTH SECOND STAGE BEATER *I'E KUKU*
POLYNESIA, HAWAIIAN ISLANDS
LATE 18TH- EARLY 19TH CENTURY

CATALOGUE NO. 28
BARCLOTH DECORATOR
POLYNESIA, HAWAIIAN ISLANDS
19TH CENTURY

CATALOGUE NO. 29
BARCLOTH DECORATOR
POLYNESIA, HAWAIIAN ISLANDS
19TH CENTURY

CATALOGUE NO. 30
BARCLOTH STAMP *OHEKAPALA*
POLYNESIA, HAWAIIAN ISLANDS
19TH CENTURY

CATALOGUE NO. 31
BARCLOTH STAMP *OHEKAPALA*
POLYNESIA, HAWAIIAN ISLANDS
19TH CENTURY

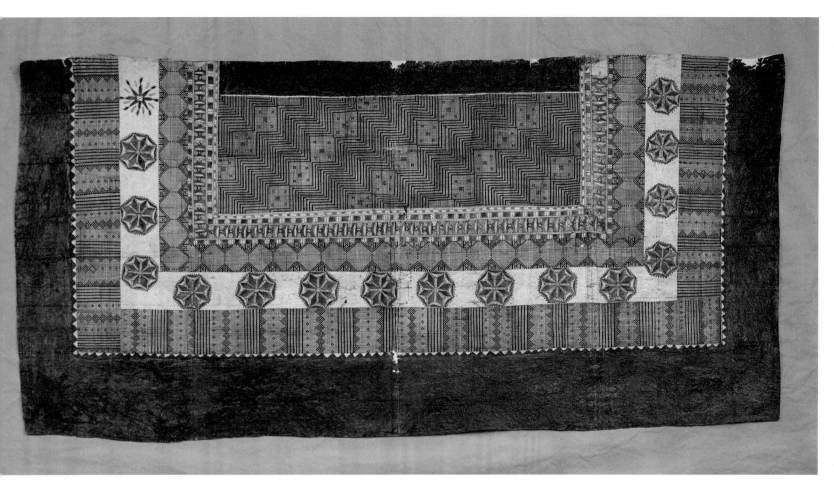

CATALOGUE NO. 32
BARKCLOTH KILT *SALATASI*
POLYNESIA, FUTUNA
19TH CENTURY

ALTHOUGH THE ISLAND CULTURES OF THE PACIFIC ARE SURROUNDED BY WATER AND ON larger islands closely circumscribed by hostile neighbors, nearly all of the inhabitants engage in trade and barter. Polynesian and Micronesian peoples have a long tradition of voyaging both for discovery and for trade. The Melanesians, who mostly live on the larger Pacific islands and archipelagoes, also have extensive trading relationships, many of which transcend long-standing hostilities.

Such geo-local materials as fish, yams, salt, powdered lime, betel nut, coconuts, quarried stone, feathers, shells, and manufactured materials including ornaments, weapons, foodstuffs, and canoes, all found their place in trade and exchange relationships.

Writing about Hawaiian fishermen, *lawai'a,* Hiroa notes their reliance on being able to purchase their *koa,* hardwood canoes from "upland" people, who lived away from the shore in the forested areas. They were also reliant on the upland people for *olana* fiber lines and nets that they made in exchange for substantial portions of the catch. (1964 [1957], vol. VII:286). The Hawaiian trolling lure in the collection embodies this relationship between sea and forest dwellers with its shell platform and its *olana* fiber binding.

Throughout Melanesia, Micronesia, and Polynesia, some ornaments were valued highly because they were constructed of material not local to their place of use. Prestige materials worn as ornament might also function as currency, especially in Melanesian societies. Certain ornaments incorporating feathers, turtle shell, cowries, boar tusks, dog incisors, and whale teeth were used in this way.

In New Zealand, the Maori on South Island bartered quarried and expertly worked jade for agricultural products with the Maori inhabitants of more temperate and fertile North Island (Barrow, 1973). Some trading activities, such as the *Kula* exchange in the Massim region, became ceremonial institutions over a wide area.

In mixed cultural locations like the Solomon Islands or the Fiji and Tonga area, the Micronesian or Polynesian peoples were acknowledged to be the best boat builders and navigators by their Melanesian neighbors. This important skill was frequently bartered for highly valued *kava* root, red feather currency, brides, and land rights.

CATALOGUE NO. 33
ADZ *TOKI*
POLYNESIA, COOK ISLANDS, MANGAIA
EARLY 19TH CENTURY

CATALOGUE 34
ADZ *TOKI*
POLYNESIA, COOK ISLANDS, MANGAIA
EARLY 19TH CENTURY

detail
CATALOGUE 34

Kava or *yaquona* drinking is a specifically Polynesian custom, both a religious practice and a secular social activity. The *kava* beverage was produced by infusing masticated shreds of the root with water, usually in a large, footed bowl, of which Catalogue No. 61 is a particularly beautiful old example. The *kava* root was not only an important commodity but also a highly prized ceremonial gift.

The Fijian club in the collection inlaid with, probably, Tongan whale ivory is an example of a cultural mixture involving trade. Tonga was a Fijian source for prized sperm whale teeth and whalebone before the advent of the Euro-American whalers. Their contributions of canoe building, ivory working, and their willingness to fight as mercenaries, enabled them to make considerable inroads into Fijian culture. When the foreign whalers and other traders came to Fiji, they found a ready market for sperm whale teeth, which became indispensable as prestige gifts, bribes, bride wealth, and ceremonial offerings for a wide variety of occasions. Mariner, who spent four years in Tonga, wrote:

In the Fiji Islands, whales' teeth are held, if possible in still greater estimation; for it would be dangerous for a man, unless he be a great chief, and even then if he were a foreigner, to be known to have a whale's tooth about him. The personal possession of such valuable property would endanger his life (Martin, 1827, vol. I:253).

When outsiders initially arrived on the Pacific islands, they found a ready market for many of the things they brought, joining a centuries-old complex of trade and barter. And even though they were encountering many cultures for the first time, they often met indigenous people who were familiar with distant islands that the foreign voyagers had only just "discovered" or were yet to "discover."

Some of the native people served the foreign voyagers as guides and interpreters in their wider travels. These guides also participated in trade and often were important advisors as to what trade goods might be highly valued in prospective landfalls. Many indigenous commodities or object types were already highly valued or had potential to become desirable trade goods over a wide area of the Polynesian triangle. For example, we know that carvings from Easter Island were exchanged with Tahitians and that Tahitian barkcloth was highly valued by Polynesian peoples of other islands in the late 18th century. The smaller Tahitian *ahufara* in the collection, Catalogue No. 54, was probably made specifically to be a ceremonial gift to a visitor.

For almost a century after first contact, Fiji remained an important source for a wide variety of ships' provisions including timber, as a locus for sandalwood and *beche le mer* for the China trade, and later for its copra production. On the other side of the equation, sperm whale teeth, glass beads, axes, knives, firearms, gunpowder, and even whaleboats were imported into Fiji. The collection has a fine selection of Fijian material culture objects, especially war clubs and barkcloth, many examples of which were obtained in this process of trade.

Another large Polynesian island location, New Zealand, was also a source for raw materials and foodstuffs, including flax, hogs, timber, and the yields of onshore whaling stations, especially in the Bay of Islands. Maori arts and crafts were also sought by and traded with visitors. Weapons, carvings and even preserved tattooed heads, like Catalogue No. 24, formed a part of the early exports upon which the Maori relied to offset their own requirements for imported goods including metal tools, dry goods, firearms, and ammunition.

The beginning of sustained contact with many Polynesian cultures at the end of the 18th century had mixed consequences for the indigenous people. A positive result was the availability of iron and steel tools, with which they produced carved trade goods of an exceptionally high quality. Notable examples of the trade goods produced in this period are the elaborately carved wooden paddles, Catalogue Nos. 5, 6, and 7, from the Austral Islands and the stone adzes, Catalogue Nos. 33 and 34 from Mangaia, Cook Islands. These finely crafted objects are well represented in the collection. These object types have been termed "ceremonial" however, aside from their possible display in festivities greeting tourists or other visitors, no specific function or meaning in indigenous ceremony or ritual has been recorded and it seems certain that they were made for trade and exchange.

The association of adzes and paddles with the Polynesian themes of canoe building and propulsion made them perfect souvenirs and mementos for cultural outsiders such as missionaries, whalers, or explorers. Recycling the once valuable stone adze blades into the trade and commerce network was a perfect solution for the Cook Islanders, as was the carving of paddles with the designs of older traditional objects for the Austral Islanders.

Contact with Euro-Americans facilitated both the availability and the movement of valuable commodities via traditional and newly created networks. Trade cloth, glass, and ceramic ornaments were incorporated rapidly, frequently being given preference over, or even replacing, indigenous materials. The Hawaiian necklace, *lei niho palaoa*, and the Marquesan ear ornament, *ha akai*, are examples of the prestige objects of marine ivory, probably obtained from foreigners.

Encounters between outsiders and Pacific islanders increased dramatically toward the end of the 18th, and were in full force by the early 19th century. Missionaries, whalers, explorers, and casual tourists alike made it a point to acquire examples of these objects in the early 19th century when the islanders produced them in quantity. The indigenous production of goods was crucial throughout the Pacific islands to support the burgeoning trade with visitors for an ever-expanding list of desirable new foreign imports.

CATALOGUE 35
COVERED BOX *WAKAHUIA*
POLYNESIA, NEW ZEALAND, MAORI
EARLY 19TH CENTURY

CATALOGUE NO. 36
CLUB *TAIAHA*
POLYNESIA, NEW ZEALAND, MAORI
EARLY 19TH CENTURY

CATALOGUE NO. 37
STILT STEP
POLYNESIA, MARQUESAS ISLANDS
LATE 18TH- EARLY 19TH CENTURY

CATALOGUE NO. 38
BARKCLOTH *MASI BOLABOLA*
POLYNESIA, FIJI, CAKAUDROVE DISTRICT
19TH CENTURY

BARKCLOTH

PLAITING AND TWINING ARE COMMON THROUGHOUT MELANESIA, MICRONESIA AND Polynesia. Basketry containers, fans, mats, sails, sunscreens, helmets, and ceremonial regalia were frequently constructed using these techniques. Natural fibers, most commonly coconut fiber, are worked into cordage for use in fishing, rigging, house construction, and personal equipment.

Finely woven belts and other fiber products were prestige objects as well as items of decoration and apparel in the Pacific islands. The collection includes woven belts from Micronesia, the earliest of these are woven purely of banana fiber and dyed in contrasting shades. Others of later manufacture incorporate colored trade yarn.

Although loom weaving was prevalent in Micronesia, Polynesian peoples relied upon beaten barkcloth, especially for use as apparel and bedding. (The notable exceptions are the Maori and the Moriori of New Zealand who, at the time of earliest contact, utilized principally twined cloaks and other garments of flax.)

The Museum has a rich collection of traditional Polynesian barkcloth. Tahiti, Fiji, Tonga, Samoa, Futuna, and the Hawaiian Islands are particularly well represented. Barkcloth was made predominantly from the macerated inner bark of the paper mulberry, although breadfruit, *ficus*, and other species are employed in some cases. Both the delicacy and the durability of these fabrics are suprising, especially considering that they were not designed by their creators to endure for decades and certainly not for centuries.

Types of barkcloth varied with intended use; heavy material with thick applications of water-repellent gum constituted an ideal rain cloak, whereas, soft, delicate fiber was fashioned into garments intended to be worn close to the skin and made into bedding. In Hawaii these large pieces were frequently colored with pink, blue and purple dyes.

Decorations varied with cultural art styles and according to the status of the user and intended use. Some of the most sacred cloth, used to wrap god figures or to mark religious enclosures, was pure white and undecorated. Marks of the beater, *i'e kuku*, may be seen in low relief on thin and otherwise undecorated *kapa* from the Hawaiian Islands.

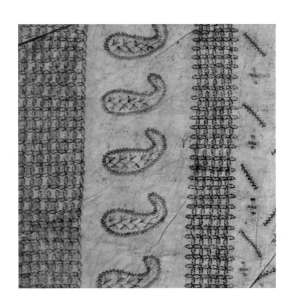

detail
CATALOGUE NO. 62

The production of barkcloth in Polynesia was an outlet for female creative expression. Traditionally, among Hawaiian and Tahitian women, those of highest status were expected to produce the finest cloth. Designs were often personal or signified certain families or lineages. Thus the process of barkcloth production also constituted a nexus for social interaction as groups of women spent long hours together engaged in beating the fabric and applying decoration. Men, too, produced barkcloth in a few locations, notably Easter Island and the Marquesas Islands. They also produced the plain barkcloth that was used for religious purposes in Tahiti, according to Ellis: *Though the native cloth worn by the inhabitants was made by the women, there were some kinds used in the temples, in the service of their idols, which were made by men, and which it was necessary, according to the declarations of the priest, should be beaten during the night* (1931: vol. I, 184).

Among the earliest and rarest barkcloths in the collection are two Tahitian shawls, *ahufara*, Catalogue Nos. 39 and 54. Each is partially decorated with delicate patterns made by printing dye-soaked flowers, leaves, and ferns. Irregular bands and rectangular areas were also dyed in variegated stripes; the smaller *ahufara* also has a rectangular collage panel, once bright red, in its center. Barkcloth of this type was produced, given ceremonially, and worn by the *ali'i*, or highest class of the society. Highly valued at their time of manufacture, these shawls were probably gifts in exchange rituals characteristic of 18th and early 19th century Tahitian society.

Perhaps the most remarkable example in the Museum's collection is a large rectangular cloth printed with fine paisley *boteh* designs evidently inspired by those on imported Indian, Kashmir, or Afghan textiles. Mrs. Hiram Bingham, wife of one of the first New England missionaries to the Hawaiian or Sandwich Islands as they were then called, is believed to have collected it during her sojourn there.

The printing on this and some other Hawaiian barkcloth of the early 19th century period was produced using bamboo splints, *ohe kapala*, each carved with a specific design element at one end. These small units were impressed on the sheet of *kapa*, sometimes in contrasting colors, to produce complex designs.

Kapa decorated with designs printed using *ohe kapala* are found in collections worldwide. Hawaiian artists developed this technique of printing shortly after foreign visitors brought printed cloth to the Islands in the late 18th century. The extraordinary paisley-patterned cloth collected by Mrs. Hiram Bingham, however, is believed to be unique. It is an excellent illustration not only of Hawaiians' innovative technology, but also of changing taste and art style in response to contact with foreign goods from a very early period.

Visitors to the Polynesian islands were impressed with the fineness of the barkcloth that they found there. The material was highly valued for presentation and trade. Indeed, many of the examples that have survived from this early contact were undoubtedly gifts to European voyagers from individuals of high status. Voyagers discovered that the finest barkcloth was esteemed over a wide area. Material collected at one port of call might be appreciated by and was sometimes used in trade with the indigenous inhabitants of another, distant island.

The islanders on their side valued European woven and printed cloth. Red feathers and the color red itself was associated with the *ali'i* entitled class in Polynesia and therefore red cloth was at a premium. Trade cloth eventually supplanted the traditional use of barkcloth for apparel in nearly all the Polynesian islands with the exceptions of Fiji, Samoa, Tonga, and the Wallis and Futuna group.

The Museum's collection includes an excellent selection of barkcloth from Tonga, Fiji, and Samoa dating from the early 19th century up to the *siapo* revival era of the 20th century in Samoa. There are dramatic Fijian black-on-white stencil designs as well as the mellower Samoan brown and beige palette, some of which were produced by the technique of rubbing the cloth over a pattern board to produce repeating geometric imagery. Other widely used decoration techniques included overall coloration, printing, and hand-painting. Perhaps the most intricate example of freehand decoration occurs on the 19th century barkcloth kilt *salatasi*, Catalogue No. 32, from Futuna.

Hawaiians and some other groups went through a brief transitional period when barkcloth was used to make western-style garments: vests, dresses, and other apparel were tailored from this material. The textile proved too fragile to be sewn, cut, and seamed as cloth could be. Subsequently, barkcloth was replaced by cotton, linen, silk, and other imported textiles.

After the first few decades of the early 1800s, the making of barkcloth died out in the Hawaiian Islands as it did in many other Polynesian islands. An effort is presently under way to study and to revive Hawaiian barkcloth technology and traditions of design, as they had been in Samoa during the mid-20th century.

Contemporary production of barkcloth in Polynesia is almost entirely geared toward outsiders' consumption, although its traditional use has continued to flourish in a few areas, notably Tonga and Fiji. Barkcloth is still valued there for ceremonial presentation and use on important occasions, as well as being made for sale to tourists.

CATALOGUE NO. 39

BARKCLOTH CAPE *'AHU FARA*

POLYNESIA, TAHITI

CIRCA 1790S

CATALOGUE NO. 40
HEADREST *KALI LALONI* OR *KALI TOLONI*
POLYNESIA, TONGA OR FIJI
19TH CENTURY

CATALOGUE NO. 41
HEADREST *KALI LALONI* OR *KALI TOLONI*
POLYNESIA, TONGA OR FIJI
LATE 18TH- EARLY 19TH CENTURY

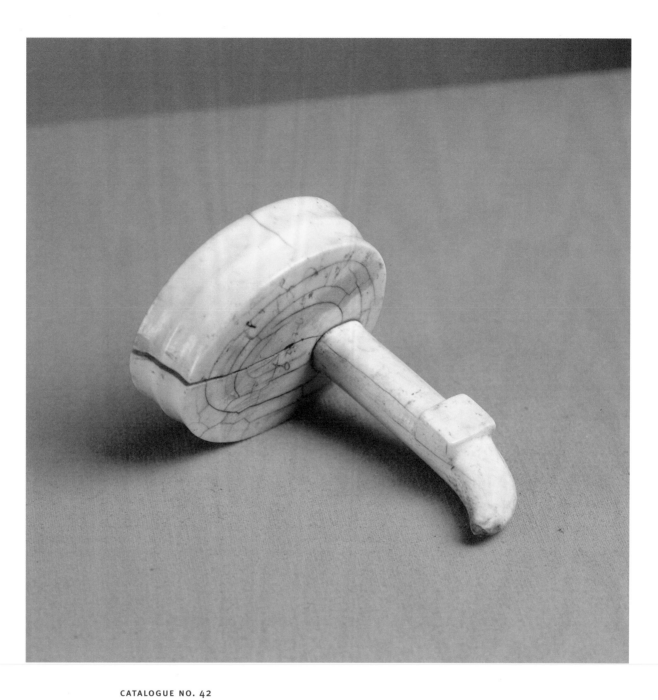

CATALOGUE NO. 42
EAR ORNAMENT *HA AKAI*
POLYNESIA, MARQUESAS ISLANDS
19TH CENTURY

CATALOGUE NO. 43
BARKCLOTH *MASI* OR *SEYAVU*
POLYNESIA, FIJI
19TH CENTURY

from back to front

CATALOGUE NO. 44
THROWING CLUB / *ULA TAVATAVA*
POLYNESIA, FIJI
EARLY 19TH CENTURY

CATALOGUE NO. 45
THROWING CLUB / *ULA TAVATAVA*
POLYNESIA, FIJI
19TH CENTURY

CATALOGUE NO. 46
THROWING CLUB / *ULA TAVATAVA*
POLYNESIA, FIJI
19TH CENTURY

CATALOGUE NO. 47
THROWING CLUB WITH IVORY INLAY
KOLO OR *ULA*
POLYNESIA, TONGA OR FIJI
19TH CENTURY

CATALOGUE NO. 48
ROUND HEADED THROWING CLUB /
ULA DRISIA
POLYNESIA, FIJI
EARLY 19TH CENTURY

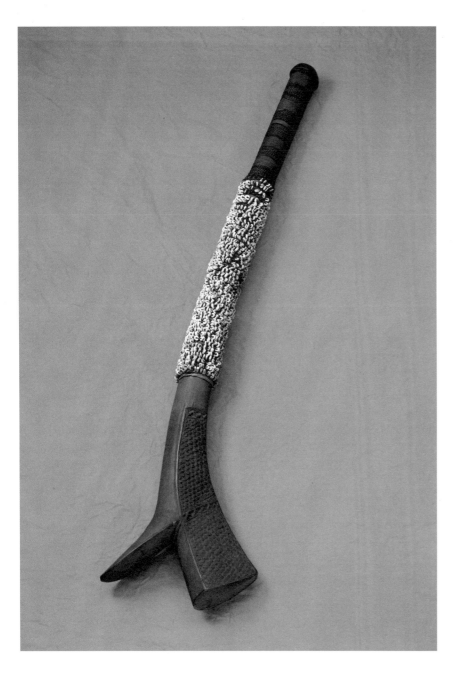

CATALOGUE NO. 49

CLUB *SALI*

POLYNESIA, FIJI

LATE 18TH- EARLY 19TH CENTURY

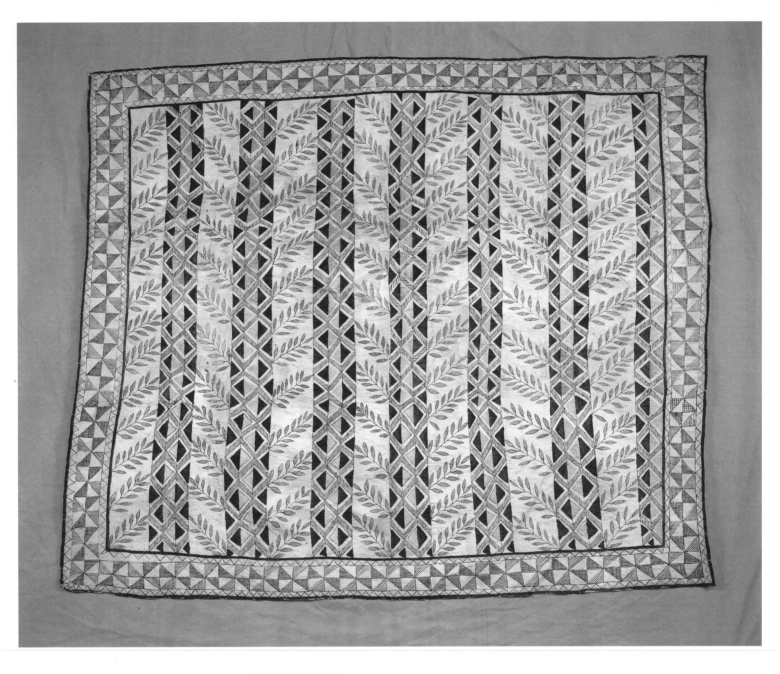

CATALOGUE NO. 50
BARKCLOTH *SIAPO MAMANU*
POLYNESIA, SAMOA,
FIRST QUARTER 20TH CENTURY

TECHNOLOGY

ALTHOUGH THE PEOPLES OF THE PACIFIC ISLANDS EVOLVED REMARKABLY SOPHISTICATED material cultures, until the time of contact with outsiders they depended upon technologies and materials derived from their insular surroundings to provide for food, shelter, transportation, warfare, and ceremony. The Museum of Natural History's collection provides many excellent examples of these remarkable technological achievements, especially from Polynesian and Micronesian cultures.

Wood was the basic raw material for the manufacture of most houses, canoes, weapons, eating utensils, and other implements. In pre-contact Polynesia, carpentry and carving was done almost entirely with stone or shell adzes. Basalt blades of diverse sizes show a surprising continuity of design over a wide area. Lashed to wooden hafts with delicately wrought bindings of coconut fiber and cushioned with shark skin or bark cloth padding, these implements are elegant and beautiful as well as having been most effective, as the creations of traditional carvers testify.

Ubiquitous shark teeth augmented the stone and shell blades. A single large shark tooth could be mounted in a wooden handle to make a simple but elegant weapon or tool. Sand, shark or ray skin, and pumice, where available, furnished the necessary abrasives for finish work. Liberal applications of coconut oil completed the simple suite of the typical workbench prior to the advent of foreign materials.

Captain Wilson, one of the first prolonged visitors to a Micronesian culture, observed after his stay in Palau: ...*a country where no aid could be obtained from the assistance of iron tools, and where every thing which was convenient and useful could only be produced by much time, labor, and patience, and at last fashioned by such poor means as necessity, stimulating invention by slow degrees brought about, it will not be expected that their domestic implements would be numerous...*

Their best knives were formed of a piece of the large mother of pearl oyster-shell, ground narrow, and the outward side a little polished. – The sort more common was made of a piece of some muscle-shell, or of split bamboo, which they sharpen to an edge, and render exceedingly serviceable...Their hatchets...the blade part being made of the strongest part of the large Kima Cockle, ground to a sharp edge (Keate, 1789: 310 - 12).

CATALOGUE NO. 51
FAN
POLYNESIA, COOK ISLANDS,
PROBABLY RAROTONGA
19TH CENTURY

He adds significantly: *But they were happy to adopt iron, when it had been given to them.*

The induction of metal into indigenous technology was accomplished during the three voyages of Captain James Cook and others as early as the 1770s. Examining the carved hardwood clubs and other implements in the collection one cannot fail to be impressed by the quality of workmanship that was achieved using even the most basic of these tools. With care, evidence of the technological changes, the availability first of soft iron, then of steel blades, can be discerned in some productions. John Mariner, who lived on Tonga for several years beginning in 1805, spoke of Tongan craftsmen's skill in cutting sperm whale teeth using newly imported, albeit crude, metal tools:

...it is astonishing with what neatness they do this, making as little waste as it would be possible to do with much better instruments than what they possess—nothing indeed but a common shaped European chissel [sic], or a piece of a saw, or in defect of these, a flattened nail rendered sharp (Martin, 1827, Vol I: 250-1).

Coconut and other vegetal fibers were employed for fishing lines, bindings, house construction, thatching, plaiting, matting, textile, and barkcloth production. Matting and twining was practiced over a wide area. String bags were produced by women of Papua New Guinea, another example of the diversity of Pacific islands textile production.

Loom weaving is a cultural attribute of Micronesian peoples and the Museum's collection includes a fine representative group of belts and related textile products, woven using a "back-strap" loom. Diverse examples, collected from early 19th to mid-20th century, furnish an interesting range of materials and designs from this region.

Pacific peoples subsisted on a predominantly vegetable diet, consisting especially of yams and taro, augmented by fish and shellfish. Chickens, pigs, and dogs were also consumed on special occasions and eaten ceremonially. On larger islands there is typically more variety however, even in the interior of New Guinea, yams, sago palms and grubs are relied upon heavily for daily nutrition even today.

Fishing is an important activity for most island dwellers. Where possible, fish were trapped, netted, speared, or poisoned. Using a wide variety of tackles and techniques, angling was also a widespread activity. The collection has an interesting array of fishing apparatus, including containers, netting, hooks, lines, and other related paraphernalia. The composite trolling lures are especially noteworthy. The barbs of bone or turtle shell are meticulously cut and ground using natural abrasives and bound to reflective shell platforms with finely twisted vegetal fiber. Intricately crafted bait hooks of bone and shell with fiber snoods, or leaders, testify to the delicate craftsmanship of their creators.

Canoe building and sailing were crucial activities, especially for Polynesian and Micronesian peoples as they enabled access to the sea, reefs, and lagoons. Most of the craft destined for ocean and tidal areas were equipped with outriggers or were actually double hulled for stability.

Polynesians and, to some extent, Micronesian peoples constructed large seaworthy vessels with hewn planks stitched together with coconut fiber and sealed using breadfruit sap or putty nut adhesive. The largest craft, over 100 feet in length, could accommodate over 200 passengers. Such huge native craft were among the scores of vessels that greeted Captain James Cook in Tahiti, matching the length of his own ships.

In New Zealand also, where there were huge trees, hulls of 100 feet in length might be dug out of a single trunk without requiring structural seams or joints. The Maori paddled coasting canoes of this length without benefit of sail or outrigger.

Canoes of all sizes were employed in a range of activities including fishing, trading, transportation, wars of conquest, and the mass migrations that brought the Polynesian and Micronesian ancestors of today's peoples to the most far-flung Pacific islands. Precisely how they made such long voyages without benefit of compass, sextant, or log is still debated. That they relied upon careful observation of the stars, water currents and temperatures, wind and wave directions, as well as flora and fauna observed along the way is indisputable.

Melanesian peoples, though canoe builders and sailors, were less daring and seldom ventured out of sight of land. On larger islands, especially New Guinea, canoes were used extensively for transportation on lakes and rivers.

Early visitors to these isolated islands were impressed with the beauty and complexity of the material culture created using what were judged to be very primitive technologies. The inhabitants, in their turn, marveled at the visitors' technological wares and were quick to adopt knives, axes, scissors, fire arms, cloth, and many other accouterments of Western civilization. As they became available these new tools and materials were quickly integrated into the cultures, frequently in ingenious ways.

Thus some of the early donors to the Providence Franklin Society made their gifts not only as specimens of "natural history" or "curiosities" from far off places, but also as relics of rapidly transforming, perhaps even vanishing, traditional cultures and technologies. By 1819, the traditional kapu and religious system of native Hawaiians was abolished by King Kamehameha II and all "idols" were ordered destroyed. A few decades after James Cook's arrival in the Hawaiian Islands, Honolulu had become a bustling port town. Imported technologies, foreign trade goods from Europe and Asia, and foreign customs were being appropriated by native Hawaiians who could afford them (Jenkins, 1989:10-15).

detail
CATALOGUE NO. 60

CATALOGUE NO. 52
CLUB *KINIKINI*
POLYNESIA, FIJI
LATE 18TH- EARLY 19TH CENTURY

CATALOGUE NO. 53
CLUB *CULACULA*
POLYNESIA FIJI
EARLY 19TH CENTURY

CATALOGUE NO. 54
SHAWL OR CLOAK *AHUFARA*
POLYNESIA, TAHITI
CIRCA 1800-1820

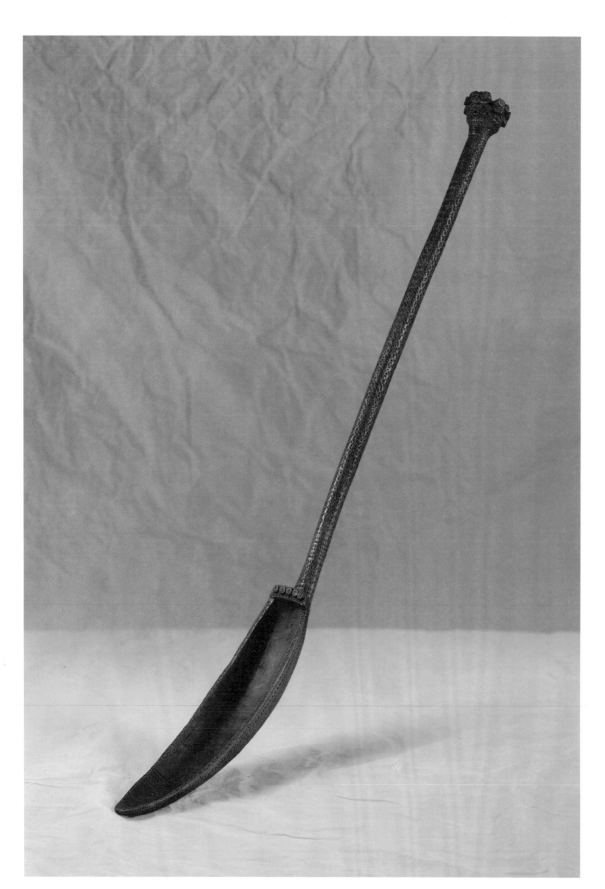

CATALOGUE NO. 55
SCOOP OR LADLE
POLYNESIA, AUSTRAL ISLANDS, RA'IVAVAE
EARLY 19TH CENTURY

from top to bottom

CATALOGUE NO. 56
TROLLING LURE FOR BONITO *PA HI AKU*
POLYNESIA, HAWAII
19TH CENTURY

CATALOGUE NO. 57
TROLLING LURE FOR BONITO *PAATU*
POLYNESIA, SAMOA
19TH CENTURY

CATALOGUE NO. 58
TROLLING LURE FOR BONITO *PAATU*
POLYNESIA, SAMOA
19TH CENTURY

CATALOGUE NO. 59
FISH HOOK AND SNOOD
POLYNESIA, TAHITI
19TH CENTURY

CATALOGUE NO. 60
FORK
POLYNESIA, FIJI
EARLY 19TH CENTURY

CATALOGUE NO. 61

BOWL *TANO'A*

POLYNESIA, TONGA

19TH CENTURY

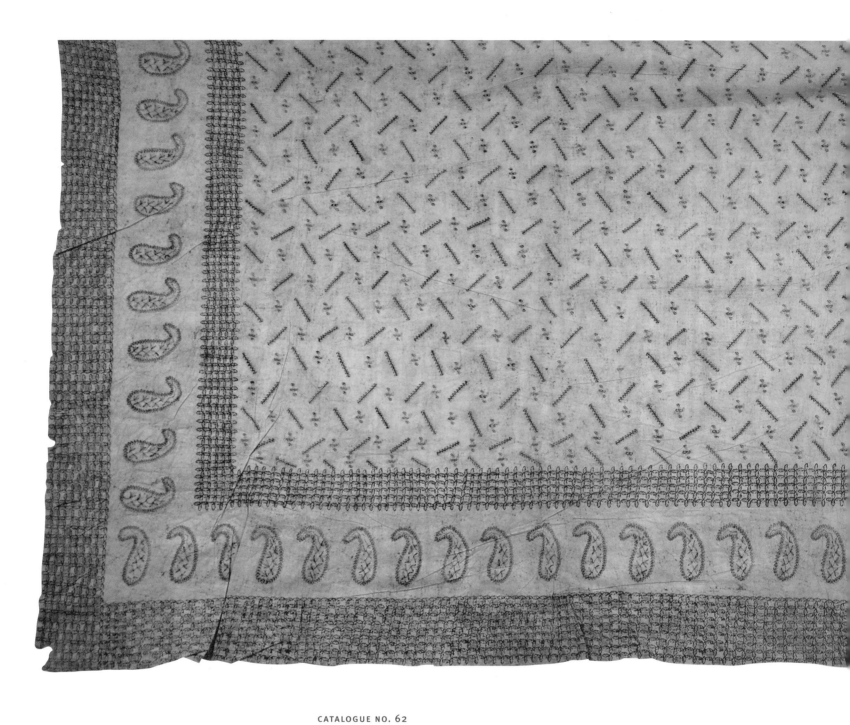

CATALOGUE NO. 62

BARKCLOTH *KAPA*

POLYNESIA, HAWAIIAN ISLANDS

EARLY 19TH CENTURY

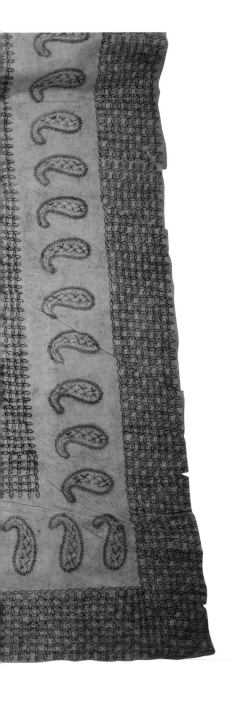

CATALOGUE NO. 64
CLUB
POLYNESIA, TONGA
19TH CENTURY

CATALOGUE NO. 64
CLUB *BOWAI*
POLYNESIA, FIJI
19TH CENTURY

CATALOGUE NO. 65
CLUB *MOUNGALAULAU*
POLYNESIA, TONGA
18TH-19TH CENTURY

FRONTISPIECE AND BACK FLYLEAF
SUPPORT FIGURE
POLYNESIA, HAWAIIAN ISLANDS
EARLY 19TH CENTURY   E2733
WOOD WITH DARK PIGMENT HIGHLIGHTS, EYES
INLAID WITH SHELL HEIGHT 39.4 CM
DONATED TO THE PROVIDENCE FRANKLIN SOCIETY BY
DANIEL TILLINGHAST ABORN BETWEEN 1829 AND 1831

In the corpus of Hawaiian sculpture, figures occur in debased postures supporting eating bowls, drinking cups, drums, *konane* boards, spittoons, and waste bowls as well as fishing pole brackets like the present example (Starzecka, 1975: 39-40 and Brigham, 1906: figs. 13-14). The style of these carvings and the attitudes of support figures are usually dramatic and in many cases involve acrobatic contortions that were characteristic of the impish folk *menehune*, and were undoubtedly meant to amuse their owners and other onlookers.

It is believed that support figures were also frequently representations of enemies or rivals. Kane suggests that the darkened face of the present example may have been created to "caricature a specific person whose face has been heavily tattooed" (letter to the author, Dec. 11, 1996).

Mack writes: *The figures, carved in servile positions, did not represent gods, but rather vanquished enemies. It was not unusual to defile the memory of dead enemies by relegating their likenesses to such menial tasks as forever supporting the victor's bowl–an extreme insult (1982: 36).*

The carver of the Museum's support figure departs somewhat from the secular, acrobatic posture of most of those cited above. The anatomical proportions and figural style closely parallel an *amakua* figure from the collection of James Hooper. This figure was collected in 1825 (Phelps, 1976: 71).

In 1819 King Kamehameha II (Liholiho) decreed the abolition of the Hawaiian *kapu* system and ordered the destruction of all religious images (Kuykendall, 1980 [1938], vol. I: 69). It is extremely unlikely that anyone would have dared to create secular sculpture that might cross the line or even mock Hawaiian religious art style, as the present example seems to do, before this iconoclastic period.

It may not be coincidental that both the present example and the Hooper Collection figure were collected in the 1820s. The support figure appears to derive from the style of the Hooper religious carving, with blocky extremities and broad feet. It is posed in a formal, while somewhat dramatic, attitude unlike religious or *amakua* images. The figure stands with his left arm raised in an exaggerated gesture, facilitating its subservient, supportive function. Based upon the proximity of collection dates and the stylistic similarities, it is possible that the same carver, or a close follower, may have created both

the Hooper carving for religious, and the present example for secular purposes within a relatively short period of time.

The dramatic posture of the support figure may also be the result of outside influence. Brigham suggests the influence of ships' figureheads on Hawaiian carvers and even the tutoring of Hawaiians by foreign carvers during the transitional period following the abolition of the *kapu* system (1906: 9 [171]). Indeed, figureheads placed below the bowsprit were frequently created in postures whose gestures seemed to support or guide the vessel. Such an attitude may have informed the creation of the present example.

The context of production of this figural bracket has unfortunately been lost. However, it clearly belongs to a period of creative florescence, stimulated in part by foreign influence and technology, during which many of the most interesting and important objects in the Museum of Natural History's collection were created.

The donor of this object and many others in the collection, Daniel Tillinghast Aborn, was a native of the Hawaiian Islands. He was born to New England parents in Hawaii on September 2, 1790, and died on Oahu in 1836. He appears to have owned interests in several ships, and may have captained one or more of them. Aborn apparently visited his parents homeland several times and donated several objects to the Providence Franklin Society on at least one of these occasions. For an extensive reconstruction of Aborn's biography and connection to Rhode Island, see Johnson (1997) and Lamar (1997).

CATALOGUE NO. 1
ARCHITECTURAL SUPPORT FIGURE
POLYNESIA, MARQUESAS ISLANDS
PROBABLY EARLY TO MID-19TH CENTURY   E3112
EXTREMELY HARD WOOD (POSSIBLY BREADFRUIT)
PIGMENT 166.97 X 22.86 CM
BROWN UNIVERSITY, APRIL 20, 1954

Large scale Polynesian sculpture is rare. This wooden post figure is among only a few such carvings to have survived from the Marquesas Islands. For three others see Von den Steinen (1969 [1928]: 99-100). The present example is the only one known to the writer that has retained its decorative surface pigmentation.

Post figures are somewhat more elongated in form than are stone effigies, which tend to be relatively compact and stocky. This variation probably relates to the form of the materials of construction, i.e. tree trunks versus boulders. Figures are always male, the postures and facial features of both are similar: face forward with large eyes, flexed legs, and hands usually placed symmetrically on their abdomens.

Like other post figures, this one wears a diadem or crown. He stands upon slightly flexed, separated legs, his lower calves merging with the circular base of the post. This latter feature is common to other Marquesan sculpture, whose feet are almost never delineated.

The post figure has three-dimensional projecting ears that are perforated and presumably once held ornaments. Anatomical details and body tattoo are highlighted with yellow pigment. The upper portion of the post is painted with a checkered pattern that also occurs on stilt poles. This treatment is reminiscent of fiber designs on drums and decorative bindings on other objects (Von den Steinen 1969 [1928]: 124, 129).

The square cut apertures in the ear lobes, together with the uneven excavations beneath the figure's arms, point to a period of execution predating the ready availability of steel tools, especially the brace and bit. The small eye orbits and the bared teeth are also characteristic of the art style of the early contact period.

That this object was made for traditional architectural use is evident from the substantial base below and notched support shaft above, which was obviously intended to receive an architectural cross member. The overall height of the object, 166.37 cm, is only a little more than twice the figure height of 65 cm.

Post figures were important vehicles for creative expression in Polynesian cultures during the pre- and early post-contact period, especially in New Zealand, the Society Islands, and the Marquesas Islands. Rather than depicting well-known gods in the Polynesian pantheon, it is likely that these sculptures represent the deified ancestors of local chiefs whose spirits might be summoned to inhabit them on important occasions.

CATALOGUE NO. 2

LIZARD FIGURE *MOKO*

POLYNESIA, EASTER ISLAND, *RAPA NUI*

LATE 18TH- EARLY 19TH CENTURY   E1910

WOOD 27.31 X 7.62 CM

DONATED BY MRS. ABRAHAM MANCHESTER, 1927

WITH THE NOTATION: *FORMERLY PROPERTY OF HER GRANDFATHER, MOSES DAILEY, THE LAST R.I. PEQUOT. SOME OF THE FAMILY WERE SEA FARING MEN AND EVIDENTLY SECURED THESE RELICS ON WHALING VOYAGES.*

Pendant, so-called "lizard figures," *moko*, are actually a composite of anthropomorphic, reptilian, and avian attributes. These figures are usually curved, with triangular head, relief carved short arms, minimal feather tail, and a pointed extremity. Metraux states that lizard images were employed as guardians of the house. He writes that smaller figures "were hung around the necks of dancers during feasts" (1971 [1940], 265-66).

This is an old, well-worn piece; the transversely pierced lug on the nap of the neck has been broken or worn away. Like many of those recorded, the present example once had eyes inlaid with bird vertebrae rims and obsidian pupils.

A fan-shaped element carved at the base of the creature's spine recalls the avian aspect of the image and represents tail feathers as noted by Heyerdahl (1975: pl. 42-43) and Essen-Bauer (1989, cats. 22-33). The figure is smaller and less detailed than any other known example and is about two-thirds the length of the next smallest one. For a comparison of published *moko* figures of various sizes and subtypes, see Hurst (2001: 328).

The pointed tail gives evidence of much wear by its patina; the eye inlays are long since missing. The penis has been cut away and the Museum number written on the lighter scarred area. Such emasculation is frequent on "primitive art" objects from 19th century collections. For another Easter Island victim of post-collection mutilation compare the George Ortiz *kavakava* figure (Sotheby's, 1978: lot 234).

CATALOGUE NO. 3

MALE CROUCHING FIGURE

POLYNESIA, EASTER ISLAND, *RAPA NUI*

LATE 18TH- EARLY 19TH CENTURY   E3198

WOOD 20.64 X 6.98 CM

BROWN UNIVERSITY'S COLLEGE MUSEUM/JENKS MUSEUM

This figure represents a somewhat stocky male in a contracted posture, with legs and arms flexed and head tilted backward in an unnatural attitude so that the figure is oriented horizontally, directing its energy (if not actually flying) forward. The figure's arms terminate in diminutive forearms with tiny hands pronating beneath his chin as though directing the orientation of the head or performing a specific gesture of contortion, the significance of which is now lost.

The animated facial features are skillfully carved in high relief: the mouth is puckered, the nose and brows are prominent, bracket-shaped ears are carved with unusual specificity. The round, staring eyes with their raised rims show clear evidence of having once contained the customary bone and obsidian inlays. Neither primary nor secondary sexual characteristics are indicated, although the shoulders are wider than the hips and the facial features conform to those of other Easter Island male carvings, with heavy eyebrows, prominent nose, and goatee.

Though deeply cracked in several places and missing the inlays of both eyes, the figure retains much of its aesthetic impact and sculptural power. It is finely carved, of evident great age, and has stylistic features that are unique in the corpus of known carvings from Easter Island.

It is possible to delineate a small sub-category of three carvings, all of which share the crouching posture and forward head orientation. Two of these "crouching figures" are in the Peabody Essex Museum collection (E-25404 and E-13896). Both are depicted in approximately the same posture as the present example. It seems likely that the posture and attitude of all three figures is reflective of a spirit and/or a human transformation. For a comparative analysis of the three figures, see Hurst (2001: 323-25, figs. 3, 9, 10, 11). For a red pigmented stone figure from the Peabody Museum at Harvard, with related posture and a facial expression very similar to the present example, see Kjellgren (2001: cat. 23).

CATALOGUE NO. 4
MALE FIGURE *MOAI KAVAKAVA*
POLYNESIA, EASTER ISLAND, *RAPA NUI*
EARLY 19TH CENTURY   E3098
WOOD, BONE, OBSIDIAN, TRACES OF RED PIGMENT
49.53 X 12.07 CM

DONATED TO THE PROVIDENCE FRANKLIN SOCIETY IN 1835 BY CAPTAIN W. P. SALISBURY WITH THE NOTATION: *AN IDOL OF THE NATIVES OF EASTER ISLAND, PACIFIC OCEAN ALSO A LARGE WAR SPEAR AND PADDLE*

The emaciated male figures, *moai kavakava*, are the most well known of the wooden figure types from Easter Island. Their reference is uncertain— whether carved to suggest ancestral figures of another time or as representations of the more recently deceased may never be known. *Moai kavakava* figures are gaunt, slightly stooped in posture, with arms at their sides. Their disproportionately large heads have enlarged ear lobes, toothy, grimacing mouths, and wear goatees. For a thorough, detailed description of *moai kavakava* attributes, see Metraux (1971 [1940]: 251-52). For illustrations of a selection of such figures see Chauvet (1934: figs 16-36).

Moai kavakava figures collected during the early contact period, like this example, are carved from indigenous *toromiro* wood and have eyes inlaid with obsidian pupils and bird bone rims. They have a figural design, or a swirling pattern, as does the present example, carved on the top of the head. For a very similar *moai kavakava*, said to have been collected in 1864, see Mack (1982: fig. 3). The Museum's *moai kavakava* is carved in a style consistent with the best and earliest of the genre. Lacking one eye inlay, it is otherwise in very good condition.

Among the dozens of such figures in the literature, the Museum's *moai kavakava* is especially significant because of its early provenance. The writer has located fewer than ten published examples with claim to having been in Western collections prior to 1870-71 (Hurst 2001: 328). This terminal date, though somewhat arbitrary, is two to three years after the conversion of all the inhabitants to Catholicism, according to Van Tilburg as cited in Kjellgren (2001: 20).

It is certain that moai *kavakava* figures were highly valued and constituted heirloom treasure for families or lineages (Attenborough, 1990: 47). Kaeppler writes, "The importance of an object was directly linked with its owner's rank and status" (2001: 33). Thus it may be assumed that many of the pieces in Western collections became disassociated from their original owners or families *in situ*. Only then would they have been available for sale or trade to outsiders as freely as Beechey reports on a visit in 1825:

Bananas, yams, potatoes, sugar cane, nets, idols etc. were offered for sale, and some were even thrown into the boat, leaving their visitors to make what return they chose (Ward, 1967, vol. II: 232).

The donor of the Museum's *moai kavakava*, Captain W. P. Salisbury, was master of the China trade vessel Hanover from 1833 to 1838. He may have acquired this figure in a secondary location, as no record has been found to indicate that he actually visited Easter Island.

CATALOGUE NO. 5

PADDLE *HOE*

POLYNESIA, AUSTRAL ISLANDS, RA'IVAVAE

EARLY 19TH CENTURY   E2522

WOOD 116.84, 13.97 CM

DONATED TO THE PROVIDENCE FRANKLIN

SOCIETY BY DANIEL TILLINGHAST ABORN

CATALOGUE NO. 6

PADDLE *HOE*

POLYNESIA, AUSTRAL ISLANDS, RA'IVAVAE

EARLY 19TH CENTURY   E2507

WOOD 109.22, 17.15 CM

PROVIDENCE FRANKLIN SOCIETY

CATALOGUE NO. 7

PADDLE *HOE*

POLYNESIA, AUSTRAL ISLANDS, RA'IVAVAE

EARLY 19TH CENTURY   E3332

WOOD 144.78, 33.02 CM

BROWN UNIVERSITY, SAID TO HAVE BEEN FROM

THE COLLECTION OF "DR. CLUB"

Catalogue No. 7 is a large paddle with a spade-shaped blade and a round handle. The pommel with eight dancing female figures is carved in high relief. No. 5 is similar to 7, but much smaller and with only five female figures. Of special interest is the upper most section of the handle of No. 5, which contains a band of sunburst designs and several discrete rows of swags and mesh patterns of contrasting scale. No. 6 is a variant on the previous two paddles, with a slightly more angular blade shape and a rectangular pommel carved with four dancing female figures on each side and a single figure on each end.

Many visitors to the Austral Islands during the early 19th century collected finely carved wooden paddles like these examples. These *hoe* are sometimes called "ceremonial" and Phelps compares them to paddles of reduced scale that were used in traditional dances on other Polynesian islands, notably Tonga and Easter Island (1976: 145).

The carved pommels on the paddle are similar to those on chiefly staves "carried by men of rank" (Phelps, 1976: 145, cat. 648). The carved details, including the dancing figures and swag patterns, are also very similar to those on wooden drums of the pre-contact period. For two drums with such patterns believed to have been collected on Cook's second or third voyage during the 1770s, see Kaeppler (1978: 160, fig. 300-02).

The surfaces of the paddles and the handled bowl, Catalogue No. 55, are elaborated with fine detail like that found on ceremonial bowls without handles, cf. Barrow (1979: 66-68). D'Alleva also notes the occurrence of the "sunburst" and other motifs on a carved wooden lentil in the Musée de Tahiti et des îles and on one example of barkcloth in the Peabody Essex Museum (1996: 2).

There is no evidence, however, that these *hoe* had a place in any indigenous rites (D'Alleva, 1990, 8-9). Because the ritual object types mentioned above were few in number and highly valued, it is reasonable that the islanders developed hybrid forms and derivative designs to satisfy the burgeoning demands posed by whalers, traders, and travelers in the early 19th century. Unfortunately, there do not appear to be contemporary accounts that might shed further light on this adaptation of ceremonial carving to what D'Alleva refers to as "the paddle style" (1996: 2).

CATALOGUE NO. 8

BETEL NUT PESTLE

MELANESIA, PAPUA NEW GUINEA, MILNE BAY

PROVINCE, MASSIM

EARLY 20TH CENTURY   E4080B

WOOD 20.32 X 2.88 CM

DONATED BY FREDERICK L. JACKSON, FIRST MATE

ON THE SCHOONER *YANKEE*, 1933-36

Lime spatulas are used in conjunction with the consumption of betel nut, a mild narcotic consumed widely, especially in Melanesia. The nut is frequently chewed in a wrapping of pepper leaf together with powdered lime made from burning calcareous shells, which catalyzes the narcotic, enhancing its effect.

This tapering pestle with its figural finial is typical of the art style of the Massim region. The crouching anthropomorphic figure, its abstracted scrolling hands raised to its chin, is often placed on small personal objects including spatulas, staves, and pestles. The scrolling shallow relief carving is also characteristic of the decorative style of the area. For a range of such objects, including betel nut accessories, see Beran (1988: pls. 5-6, 85).

CATALOGUE NO. 9

LIME SPATULA

MELANESIA, PAPUA NEW GUINEA, MILNE BAY

PROVINCE, LOUISIADE ARCHIPELAGO

PROBABLY EARLY 20TH CENTURY   E4076

WOOD 30.48 X 5.08 CM

DONATED BY FREDERICK L. JACKSON, FIRST MATE

ON THE SCHOONER *YANKEE*, 1933-36

Although betel nut may be bitten, rolled in a leaf with lime, and chewed, older men and others with defective teeth had recourse to grinding the nut. The betel nut mortar and pestle, along with a lime container and spatula are common personal accessories throughout the regions of Melanesia where betel nut is consumed.

Spatulas and other personal implements are usually decorated with traditional motifs of the region. Finely engraved abstract designs inspired by flora and fauna are characteristic of the entire Massim area. The distinctive pinwheel-shaped finial on the handle is a design that may be localized to the D'Entrecasteaux Islands, cf. Beran (1988: 31) and Beran (1980: 18, cat. 3).

CATALOGUE NO. 10

CANOE PROW FIGURE *TOTOISHU* OR *MUSU MUSU*

MELANESIA, SOLOMON ISLANDS

19TH CENTURY   E4189

WOOD, SHELL, WHITE INLAY, DARK ADHESIVE

15.24 X 10.8 CM

DONOR UNRECORDED

Figural charms like this example were observed in the central Solomon Islands as early as 1768 by Bougainville, who described "the head of a man carved; the eyes were of mother of pearl ... the lips were stained a very bright scarlet" (as quoted in Woodford 1909: 506). Canoe prow figures were made in a range of sizes; they were attached to small canoes and to large vessels used for inter-island travel and headhunting raids. For an image of a prow figure on a large canoe loaded with paddlers embarked on such a raid, see Waite (1983: 36).

Security at sea appears to have been the purpose for these charms. Somerville reports their use "as a safeguard against the malevolent submarine water spirit, *kesoko*" (1897: 384). The figure was attached to the prow near the water line where it could directly confront the *kesoko*, who was believed to have power over "wind and water and might capsize the canoe and devour the occupants" (Hurst, 1996: 17).

The *totoishu* or *musu musu* is characterized by a domed head, prognathous features, parted lips revealing clenched teeth, and hands positioned near the chin. The pointed ears with their enlarged circular lobes are particularly notable in this example. The brow, eyes, cheeks, and jaw are inlaid with curved pieces of shell and white pigment, a frequent decorative embellishment on carvings in the Central and Eastern Solomon Islands. A lug at the back with two square-cut apertures would have facilitated its attachment to the canoe.

Although no collection history is available for the present example, its surface and desiccation suggest considerable age, possibly mid-19th century. The sparing use of shell inlay and the presence of square- rather than round-bored holes also reinforce this estimation.

CATALOGUE NO. 11

WEAPON *RERE* OR *BETIA*

MICRONESIA, KIRIBATI

PROBABLY LATE 19TH CENTURY   E3157

WOOD, SHARK TEETH, COCONUT FIBER, HUMAN HAIR,

LEAF, FIBER 95.88 X 52.71 CM

BROWN UNIVERSITY

CATALOGUE NO. 12

WEAPON *RERE* OR *BETIA*

MICRONESIA, KIRIBATI

19TH CENTURY   E2287

WOOD, SHARK TEETH, COCONUT FIBER, RAY SKIN,

HUMAN HAIR 50.8 X 24.13 CM

PROVIDENCE FRANKLIN SOCIETY

These shark tooth-edged, thrusting weapons are each composed of a central shaft with three shorter projecting members bound to it with coconut fiber. Catalogue No. 12 has a strip of ray skin as a part of this binding. An especially tough material, it was employed to protect the binding from being cut by contact with other weapons in combat. The teeth on Catalogue No. 11 are secured between thin strips of wood bound with coconut fiber and human hair.

Intermediate-sized weapons like these were employed as swords in hand to hand fighting. They were used in thrusting and slashing motions, especially directed at the unprotected parts of antagonists. Koch mentions underarms and stomachs of foe as being particularly popular targets (1965: 197). On his first encounter in what is now Kiribati [the Kingsmill Group] in 1841 Wilkes reports (1970 [1845], vol. V: 47): *The arms and legs of a large proportion of the natives exhibited numerous scars, many of which were still unhealed. These had been made with sharks-teeth swords...*

For related forms see Koch (1965: 193-37, Tafel 38) and Triede (1997: pl. 172-73, 176).

CATALOGUE NO. 13

SPEAR *SOKILAKI-VAI*

POLYNESIA, FIJI

19TH CENTURY   E2568

WOOD, FIBER, BARKCLOTH, FRAGMENTARY

STINGRAY SPINES 328.59 X 5.39 CM

PROVIDENCE FRANKLIN SOCIETY

CATALOGUE NO. 14

SPEAR *TIKAU*

POLYNESIA, FIJI

EARLY 19TH CENTURY   E2567

WOOD, COCONUT FIBER 283.21 X 2.95 CM

PROVIDENCE FRANKLIN SOCIETY

CATALOGUE NO. 15

SPEAR *GADREGADRE*

POLYNESIA, FIJI

EARLY 19TH CENTURY   E3181

WOOD 267.02 X 7 CM

BROWN UNIVERSITY

CATALOGUE NO. 16

SPEAR *MOTO*

POLYNESIA, FIJI

PROBABLY EARLY 19TH CENTURY   E3179

WOOD 281.94 X 6 CM

BROWN UNIVERSITY

CATALOGUE NO. 17

SPEAR *GADREGADRE*

POLYNESIA, FIJI

19TH CENTURY   E2566

WOOD, COCONUT FIBER, SHELL 327.66 X 8.6 CM

PROVIDENCE FRANKLIN SOCIETY

CATALOGUE NO. 18

SPEAR *TIKAU*

POLYNESIA, FIJI

19TH CENTURY   E2569

WOOD, COCONUT FIBER 366.1 X 7.62 CM

PROVIDENCE FRANKLIN SOCIETY

Fijian spears were made in a variety of intricate designs and with multiple tiers of long, elaborate, curved barbs. They were carried and used in the almost continuous warfare that is known to have characterized the late 18th and first three-quarters of the 19th century. Spears were effective both to intimidate and to attack enemies.

Spears might be thrown from fortifications at assailants or thrown over fortification walls, sometimes with flaming barkcloth attached to set afire the thatch of the besieged town. The Fijian warrior learned to throw the heavy spear with great accuracy over distances exceeding fifty feet. It could also be thrown with lightning speed and tremendous force at shorter distances (Clunie, 1977: 66).

The presence of barbs would prevent the spear's being cleanly thrown through antagonists' fleshy parts. The barbs of certain spears were designed to break off in wounds, leaving jagged remnants behind to fester and cause often fatal infections. In addition to the carved wooden barbs, some spears, like Catalogue No. 13, were tipped with stingray spines, themselves particularly vicious weapons that would slide off the spear tip and remain in the wound. Stingray spines were not only used on spear tips but also alone as assassin's weapons (Clunie, 1977: 65; figs. 23, 4).

Various spear types were named for natural forms, including bamboo, stingray spines, parrot beaks. Catalogue Nos. 13 and 18 are called *tikau*, referring to the formal resemblance of the expanded elements between the barb clusters to the wild yam. Other spear types were named for their material of construction or the place they were made (Clunie, 1977: 69-70).

Spears were not only used in battle but also in ceremony and dance. They were often given a festive appearance by wrapping them with shell beads, fancy fiber bindings and barkcloth streamers. Catalogue No. 17, with its strands of shell beads and binding, is a good example of such embellishment.

CATALOGUE NO. 19

WEAPON *RERE* OR *BETIA*

MICRONESIA, KIRIBATI

19TH CENTURY   E2555

WOOD, SHARK TEETH, COCONUT FIBER, HUMAN

HAIR, RAY SKIN 262.59 CM

PROVIDENCE FRANKLIN SOCIETY

The indigenous inhabitants of Kiribati involved themselves in both inter- and intra-island combat. Not only were whole islands thus involved one against another, but also individual islands with defensive palisades around towns reaching "eight to ten feet high" (1970 [1845], vol. V: 93). Long, shark tooth-edged, pole weapons like this example extended the warriors' reach to antagonists on the battlefield and above and below fortification walls. This weapon is edged about half its length with four rows of shark teeth and four arching side elements. Wilkes reports observing similar weapons:

The spears are equally formidable, and four rows of shark's teeth are inserted in them some are of uncommon length of twenty feet, but they are usually about eight or ten feet long and have prongs projecting from their sides also armed with teeth. (1970 [1845], vol. V: 47)

CATALOGUE NO. 20

COVERED BOWL WITH SHELL INLAY

MICRONESIA, PALAU

PROBABLY LATE 19TH CENTURY   E2498

WOOD WITH RED-BROWN PIGMENT, SHELL, AND

COCONUT FIBER 24.29 X 19.69 CM

DONATED FEBRUARY 13, 1933 BY ISABEL HOWARD

DUNCAN IN MEMORY OF HER LATE HUSBAND

DR. RICHARD FRANCIS DUNCAN, (1865-1932).

CATALOGUE NO. 21

COVERED BOWL WITH SHELL INLAY

MICRONESIA, PALAU

LATE 19TH- EARLY 20TH CENTURY   E2497

WOOD WITH RED-BROWN PIGMENT, SHELL

30.48 X 36.83 CM

DONATED FEBRUARY 13, 1933 BY ISABEL HOWARD

DUNCAN IN MEMORY OF HER LATE HUSBAND

DR. RICHARD FRANCIS DUNCAN, (1865-1932).

CATALOGUE NO. 22

PLATTER *ONPAL* OR *ONGALL*

MICRONESIA, PALAU

LATE 19TH- EARLY 20TH CENTURY   E2499

WOOD WITH RED-BROWN PIGMENT, SHELL, FIBER

77.12 X 35.88 CM

DONATED FEB. 13, 1933 BY ISABEL HOWARD DUNCAN IN

MEMORY OF HER LATE HUSBAND DR. RICHARD FRANCIS

DUNCAN, (1865-1932) WITH A NOTATION THAT THE

PLATTER *BELONGED TO KING GBADOALI.*

Palau islanders used containers and platters of red-pigmented wood, often with shell inlaid designs, for ceremonial feasts and other important occasions. The pigment and finish derives from red ochre mixed with *parinarium* nut oil, according to Treide (1997: 218).

The first prolonged visit to Palau by outsiders was of Captain Henry Wilson and crew of the *Antelope*, shipwrecked there in 1783. The account, written by George Keate, mentions "wooden baskets [sic] with covers, very nicely carved and inlaid with shells. These they hung up in their houses for use and decoration" (1789: 310 and pl. 5-3).

The production and use of these vessels appears to be a long tradition, however examples of the age and quality of Catalogue Nos. 20, 21, and 22 are rare in Western collections. Although received by the Museum in the 20th century, they appear to be considerably older.

Catalogue No. 20 is an oval-shaped covered vessel inlaid with shell elements in diamond, triangle, thin rod, and "v"-shapes that produce a simple, abstract floral design. The oval lid also has a matching inlaid pattern and appears once to have had a knob or finial. For a related covered vessel with its separately carved knob, see Treide (1977: cat. 83). Catalogue No. 21 is also a covered vessel with fitted lid and inlay elements in star, cross, and "v"-forms. The concave foot rim is perforated twice on one side, probably for hanging as noted by Keate above.

Catalogue No. 22 is a shallow, elliptical-footed bowl the lateral edges of which have delicate cross-shaped inlays. Its foot rim is also perforated and it retains its fiber suspension cord. The provenance given with the platter is intriguing. Hanlon suggests that "*Gbadoali*" may be a conflation of the title of the paramount chief of Koror, Palau: "*Ibedul*." The name would be King *Ibeduhl*. This name was also spelled "*Abba Thule*" by Keate in recording Captain Wilson's account of 1783 (Feldman and Hanlon, 2002).

These vessels may be compared with examples in the collection of the Staatlichen Museums für Völkerkunde Dresden that entered that museum in the last quarter of the 19th century (Treide 1997: 218-19, cats. 8, 11, 83). Another of the Dresden vessels, a tall container for fermented beverages, *inengel* or *ilenge*, was purchased in 1929 and may be somewhat later than the others (ibid. cat. 7). It is inlaid with chips of broken porcelain rather than the customary shell.

For a group of similar objects, also reportedly from a Rhode Island collection circa 1900, see Sotheby's New York, (1986: lots 33-36). For other related traditional vessels from Japanese collections, most predating WW II, cf. Matsuoka (1927: 588-92, pls. 93, 97, 98, 99) and Kato (1997: 38-39). For still more recently manufactured examples, including a platter, *onpal* or *ongall* and a tall container for liquid, *inengel* or *ilengel* inlaid with shell, circa 1950s or later, see Wavell (1998: cats. 48, 53).

CATALOGUE NO. 23

NECKLACE

MICRONESIA, MARSHALL ISLANDS

PROBABLY 20TH CENTURY   E1583

CORAL, VEGETAL FIBER, COMMERCIAL COTTON

CORDAGE 60.96 CM

DONOR UNRECORDED

Thirty-four pairs of discoidal coral beads, bound to a plaited leaf cord with cotton cord; cotton cord tie. For a similar necklace cf. Treide (1997: cat. 43). The cited example has an elaborate pendant, however the necklace strand elements appear to be identical.

CATALOGUE NO. 24

TATTOOED HEAD *MOKOMOKAI*

POLYNESIA, NEW ZEALAND, MAORI

EARLY 19TH CENTURY   E2293

COMPLETE DRIED HEAD OF A MAN, PRESERVED

ACCORDING TO MAORI TRADITIONAL TECHNOLOGY

RETAINING HAIR, TEETH, AND SKULL, WITH THE EYELIDS SEWN SHUT

24.13 X 19.05 X 13.34 CM

PROVIDENCE FRANKLIN SOCIETY, DONATED BY CAPTAIN DANIEL ABORN, 1831

Subcutaneous injection of pigment is virtually the universal mode of tattooing in the Pacific islands and worldwide. The Maori however, were unique in the practice of carving designs into the skin of the tattooed individual; sooty pigment was placed in the fresh grooves for enhanced effect. For a clear description of the technical process and the material traditionally employed, see Robley (1896: 48-63) and Cowan (1910: 188-95).

Moko was a highly valued and costly process. Women's *moko* was usually limited to areas around the mouth, and perhaps a small area of the forehead and the pubic area. As in wider Polynesia, Maori women were traditionally tattooed to a lesser extent than men, who often decorated a high percentage of their skin.

The Maori tradition of preserving the tattooed heads of relatives and friends, as well as those of vanquished enemies, was noted by some of the earliest visitors to New Zealand. Upon death, the head of the deceased chiefly male might be removed and preserved by his clan. There is no evidence of this having been practiced on women.

The first recorded sale of a preserved head was to Joseph Banks of James Cook's expedition in 1770 (Donne, 1927: 150). Following the Maori custom of preserving and safeguarding the heads of their esteemed deceased, the displaying, taunting, and desecrating those of their foes also became prevalent. Yate records a Maori litany for taunting the preserved head of an enemy (1835: 130). Ultimately the sale of the head of a foe to a foreigner accom-

plished two ends. Its trade value could be a source for much sought-after guns and ammunition. According to Donne, such transactions were believed to transcend even the ultimate traditional insult of throwing the abused relic to one's dogs when it had outlasted its trophy and entertainment value (1927: 150-51).

Yate writes about the North Island Maori around the Bay of Plenty:

(The Maori) *formerly used to preserve the heads of their friends and keep them with religious strictness: and it was not till Europeans proposed to buy them, that the idea occurred to them of preparing the heads of their enemies; first as an article of barter, and, more recently, as a trophy of victory.* He continues, ...*the natives have ceased altogether to preserve the heads of their friends, lest by any means they should fall into the hands of others and be sold; which, of all ideas, is the one of the most horrible to them* (1835: 130-31).

The tattooing, subsequent preserving of the heads of slaves and captives, as well as the preserving of the already tattooed heads of killed or captured enemies for sale or trade, flourished in the late 18th and early 19th centuries. One canoe landed at Rangihoua in 1818, after participating in one of Hongi's notoriously successful raids, carrying 70 severed and preserved enemy heads (Smith, 1910: 95). The missionary Marsden reported subsequently seeing "stuck on poles, the preserved heads brought back from the East Coast" (ibid).

In 1831 a white trader unwittingly and imprudently displayed a group of *mokomokai* to members of the victims' families and friends, creating outrage among the local Maori people. When news of the matter reached the office of the Colonial Secretary, he ordered an end to the traffic and set fines (Robley, 1896: 178-81).

This colonial edict appears to have had some effect, but not to have totally stopped the commerce. As late as 1840 officers of the U.S. Exploring Expedition succeeded in procuring two "beautiful specimens" from the steward of a missionary brig in the Bay of Islands for ten pounds (Wilkes, 1970 [1845], vol. II: 399).

Captain Aborn donated this *mokomokai* to the Providence Franklin Society on April 4, 1831. It was undoubtedly collected before the above mentioned legislation. If one accepts Yate, as cited above, it would seem likely that the present example would have been a war trophy, taken by Maori victors and subsequently sold or traded, probably for weapons or gunpowder, in order to prosecute further warfare.

Opinions differ substantially concerning the significance and meaning of *moko*. Yate, writing in the early 19th century states:

The tattoo is no special mark of chieftanship, as has been stated by almost all writers on New Zealand: for many chiefs, of the first rank, are without a single line; others, even in old age, are only partially covered; and many a slave has had the greatest pain taken to give this ornamental operation the greatest effect upon his plebeian face. Nor do the peculiar marks on the faces of different people denote their rank, or the tribe to which they belong: it all depends upon the taste of the artist, or upon the direction of the person operated upon (1835:148).

Simmons has written extensively about the potential for interpreting Maori *moko* designs in the modern era, asserting that they contain literal information about individual identity, lineage, and other particulars (1989: 29-89). Deciphering these patterns today, over two centuries after they were created, must remain somewhat conjectural, in the writer's opinion.

Mokomokai were widely exhibited in natural history and ethnography displays during most of the 20th century. They are seldom seen in museums today and many recently published books on Maori tattoo do not even include their images. For photographic illustrations of *mokomokai* in museum collections, see Barrow (1969: pl. 28), Robley (1896: figs. 154, 164, 169, 170, 172, 174, 175, 178, and 180), and Donne (1927: 153). For a selection of period photographs and artist's renderings of living tattooed Maori men and women, see Blackburn (1999:50-67 and 70-85).

There has been a recent revival of interest in tattoo among contemporary Maori peoples who, today, use subcutaneous pigments. Some Maori tattoo artists are attempting to improve their understanding of the form and meaning of their ancestral *moko* tradition, however. For these and other individuals interested in the full range of Maori art, design, and culture, the Museum's *mokomokai* constitutes a potentially valuable resource (Niech, personal interview, Oct.4, 2000). Though nearly two hundred years of age, this tattooed head is well preserved and constitutes an excellent example of the aesthetics and workmanship that characterized the best Maori tattoo or *moko*.

CATALOGUE NO. 25
NECKLACE *LEI NIHO PALAOA*
POLYNESIA, HAWAIIAN ISLANDS
EARLY 19TH CENTURY   E2278
CARVED SPERM WHALE TOOTH, BRAIDED HUMAN HAIR,
PLANT (PROBABLY *OLANA*) FIBER
25.4 X 10.16 X 5.08 X 6.35 CM
BROWN UNIVERSITY

Royal Hawaiian pendants, *lei niho palaoa*, are well documented in the literature. The present example is remarkable for its deep color and the numerous nodules in the core of the tooth, which are revealed in the interior concavity. Pre-contact *niho* were usually much smaller and frequently made of indigenous materials such as coral, bone, or wood. The advent of whalers during the late 18th and early 19th century provided increased availability of marine ivory for the carving of *niho* pendants.

The hair of the head is believed to embody an individual's status both spiritually and symbolically. Thus necklaces and ornaments made from human hair had a corresponding high degree of significance, and were charged with a greater or lesser amount of *mana* both on account of their origins and of the status of their possessor. The Hawaiian *lei niho palaoa*, with its thick bundle of braided human hair, was both a potent chiefly object and a prestigious personal adornment. Only an *ali'i*, or person of royal birth, would have sufficient *mana* to wear such a composite necklace without harm. It would have been preserved carefully because of its value and its burden of personal *mana*. Great care would have been exercised to protect it from sorcery, contamination, or abuse.

When King Kamehameha II officially abolished the *kapu* system in 1819, pre-contact beliefs about the protection of one's *mana* diminished. At the same time, with the increasing availability of marine ivory from the whaling fleet, necklaces began to be made for foreigners. Many of these incorporated newly available materials such as silk ribbon and glass or lathe-turned ivory beads. Older necklaces were also sometimes re-stranded, replacing the human hair bundle. This process obviated any potential hazard to or from *mana* residing in the hair strands, a lingering concern to many Hawaiian people even after 1819. For examples of *niho* pendants, with and without hair strands, see D'Alleva (1990: 56); D'Alleva and Hurst (1987: 14-15); Rose (1980: cat. 197); and Mack (1982: 44-55).

CATALOGUE NO. 26

BARKCLOTH SECOND STAGE BEATER *I'E KUKU*

POLYNESIA, HAWAIIAN ISLANDS

19TH CENTURY   E3600

WOOD 39.37 X 3.49 CM

CATALOGUE NO. 27

BARKCLOTH SECOND STAGE BEATER *I'E KUKU*

POLYNESIA, HAWAIIAN ISLANDS

LATE 18TH- EARLY 19TH CENTURY   E3103

WOOD 38.74 X 4.45 CM

BISHOP MUSEUM BY EXCHANGE IN 1954

Catalogue Nos. 26 and 27 have different patterns on each of their four faces. Two surfaces of No. 26 have parallel grooves; the other two are engraved with a grid pattern on which deep concave pits are placed within each square.

Hawaiian barkcloth, *kapa*, is among the most refined and varied of all Polynesian barkcloth. Production encompassed two stages. The first stage involved processing the bark and beating it with a round faced wooden beater, *hohoa*, on a stone anvil. At the end of the first stage, barkcloth sheets might be stored for an indeterminate period.

The second stage of the process involved beating with *i'e kuku* such as these on a wooden anvil or grooved board, which further refined the cloth and imparted decorative patterns. For a discussion of Hawaiian barkcloth preparation, beaters, and examples of various patterns, see Hiroa (1964, vol. V: 169-80); Brigham (1911: pls. 1-2); and Kooijman (1972: 97-117).

CATALOGUE NO. 28

BARKCLOTH DECORATOR

POLYNESIA, HAWAIIAN ISLANDS

19TH CENTURY   E3525A

BAMBOO 29.21 X 1.91 CM

BISHOP MUSEUM BY EXCHANGE

CATALOGUE NO. 29

BARKCLOTH DECORATOR

POLYNESIA, HAWAIIAN ISLANDS

19TH CENTURY   E3525B

BAMBOO 43.18 X 1.91 CM

BISHOP MUSEUM BY EXCHANGE

The use of stamps with these delicate individualized designs to print barkcloth is a practice unique to the Hawaiian Islands. Separate components were linked to make more complex patterns, or simply repeated to create a continuous line or solid field of pattern not unlike those found in traditional

Polynesian tattoo. A chevron design is carved on the flat bamboo handle of Catalogue No. 28. For examples of other *ohekapala* and further discussion of their use, see Hiroa (1964, vol. V: 192-202), Kooijman (1972: 126-45), and Brigham (1911: 110-12).

The practice of decorating barkcloth with stamps like these appears to be a post-contact, late 18th or very early 19th century development. Whether this method of decoration emerged as a response to complex patterns seen on imported cloth, or from other influences is uncertain. The Hawaiian *kapa* artist rapidly developed a facility and ingenuity with this technique of barkcloth decoration. The large stamp-printed *kapa*, Catalogue No. 62, is a unique and extraordinary example of this innovation.

CATALOGUE NO. 30

BARKCLOTH STAMP *OHEKAPALA*

POLYNESIA, HAWAIIAN ISLANDS

19TH CENTURY   E3524A

BAMBOO 38.1 X 1.59 CM

BISHOP MUSEUM BY EXCHANGE

CATALOGUE NO. 31

BARKCLOTH STAMP *OHEKAPALA*

POLYNESIA, HAWAIIAN ISLANDS

19TH CENTURY   E3524B

BAMBOO 33.5 X .875 CM

BISHOP MUSEUM BY EXCHANGE

So-called "*kapa* liners" were used to make parallel lines on barkcloth. There has been some controversy as to whether these tools were used to print or to draw the lines. Hiroa describes their use in printing only. Kooijman states that they were used as "pens," to draw the lines; Brigham seems to agree with the latter, also calling them "pens." Brigham speaks of "marking points" and "ruling...each individual line" which suggests the use of the liners to draw rather than to print. See Hiroa (1964 [1957]: 202-05), Kooijman (1972: 128-33); and Brigham (1911: 102-04).

CATALOGUE NO. 32

BARKCLOTH KILT *SALATASI*

POLYNESIA, FUTUNA

19TH CENTURY   E3490

BARKCLOTH, PIGMENT 163.21 X 74.93 CM

HAFFENREFFER MUSEUM, 1955

The *salatasi* is a man's kilt with a black border and interior bands hand-painted in black and red pigments alternating with hatched bands and floral motifs. Decorative borders are oriented on three sides only, as the upper edge would have been folded and bound around the waist. Burrows, describing the types and the methods of production of barkcloth on Futuna in 1932, notes:

The finely decorated, black, white, and red salatasi, which is said to be the old Futunan bark-cloth kilt, has almost gone out of use (1936: 185-92).

The barkcloth from Futuna constitutes some of the finest examples of Polynesian hand-drawn design work. It has been noted that the elaborate border patterns of the *salatasi* are very similar to those woven on plaited mat loincloths from the Marshall Islands of Micronesia.

Kooijman presents three possible explanations for this proposed cross-cultural influence. First, direct invasion from the Marshall Islands, an idea supported by Futuna oral history. Second, Futuna voyagers are known to have visited Kiribati, whose inhabitants in turn traded with the Marshall Islands for arrowroot flour, preserved Pandanus fruits, fishhooks, ornaments, and probably also mats. Finally, Euro-American ships frequently visited both the Marshall Islands and Futuna and may have been a conduit for Marshall Island mats (1972: 271-82). See D'Alleva and Hurst (1987: 50) and Leonard and Terrell (30-32), where the theory of Marshall Island design influence is also noted. For other examples of *salatasi*, see Niech and Pendergrast (1998 [1997]: 63-66) and Burrows (1936: pl. 11A).

CATALOGUE NO. 33

ADZ *TOKI*

POLYNESIA, COOK ISLANDS, MANGAIA

EARLY 19TH CENTURY   E2537

STONE, WOOD, COCONUT FIBER, SHARK SKIN

93.35 X 33.02 CM

PROVIDENCE FRANKLIN SOCIETY

CATALOGUE 34

ADZ *TOKI*

POLYNESIA, COOK ISLANDS, MANGAIA

EARLY 19TH CENTURY   E2538

STONE, WOOD, COCONUT FIBER, SHARK SKIN

74.3 X 34.29 CM

PROVIDENCE FRANKLIN SOCIETY

These adzes from Mangaia, are characterized by finely ground stone blades, meticulously carved openwork pedestal handles, and delicate fiber binding. Like the decorative paddles from the Cook Islands, they were collected in considerable numbers during the early post-contact period when iron and steel blades were rapidly replacing those of stone.

These finely made but increasingly obsolete stone blades were united with the newly and elaborately carved hafts. The resulting "ceremonial" adzes rapidly entered the stream of commerce and constituted an indigenous trade item that helped to offset the ever-growing demand for foreign goods.

Catalogue Nos. 33 and 34 are excellent examples of *toki*; each has a delicate fiber binding and there is a section of sharkskin cushioning around each blade. The finely carved openwork base or haft of No. 33 is square; that of No. 34 is round in section.

The carving style on the handles of these adzes is clearly derived from that found on pre-contact religious objects, like the so-called "mace" gods characterized by rows of interconnected abstract openwork images. Cf. (Barrow (1979: 88-93, pls. 96-97, 100-01); D'Alleva (1990: 8-9); Mack (1982: 242); and Idiens (35-44).

CATALOGUE 35

COVERED BOX *WAKAHUIA*

POLYNESIA, NEW ZEALAND, MAORI

EARLY 19TH CENTURY   E3100

WOOD, RED AND BLACK STAIN 45.72 X 7.62 CM

POSSIBLY PROVIDENCE FRANKLIN SOCIETY OR

BROWN UNIVERSITY'S JENKS MUSEUM

Wakahuia are treasure boxes used to store personal valuables. According to Simmons, these were mostly objects worn on the head or neck of their chiefly owner (1984: 183). These personal ornaments, according to traditional Polynesian belief, would have carried much *mana*, or personal power. Such highly charged objects could have endangered individuals of inferior status if they chanced to come near or touch them. As a precaution against such misfortune, as well as for security, treasured objects were stored in *wakahuia*, slung from the rafters out of harm's way.

This elongated container has projecting mask lugs for suspension. The cover depicts opposed arching figures facing upward, with hands on hips and with specific male and female genitals; they undoubtedly represent an ancestral couple. The rest of the cover and box are ornamented with scrolling, shallow, relief-carved decoration painted red and black. Because the boxes were viewed from below when not being handled, they are usually richly carved on all surfaces. For examples of *wakahuia* with related copulating or paired couples on their covers, see Barrow (1969: pls. 225-32).

CATALOGUE NO. 36

CLUB *TAIAHA*

POLYNESIA, NEW ZEALAND, MAORI

EARLY 19TH CENTURY   E2285

WOOD, SHELL, ADHESIVE 172.72 X 5.08 CM

PROVIDENCE FRANKLIN SOCIETY

The *taiaha* is a ubiquitous weapon in the traditional Maori arsenal. It was carried by most chiefly men and used both as a weapon and a prestige staff. As a weapon, the spatulate blade might deliver parrying and slicing attacks. The carved head at the top of the handle was not only decorative, but also was used as a pointed thrusting weapon.

Seen from the hilt end, the carving represents the visage of a *tiki* with a defiantly outstretched tongue. The side views present differently configured heads, including that of the avian-beaked *manaia*. Like other Maori carvings, the eyes are inlaid with disks of *pahua* shell, applied not only as decorative embellishments, but also for their potential to visually distract an opponent.

Although the *taiaha* persisted in manufacture and use well into the 19th century, it appears to have constituted a status object, being used for ceremonial fencing, and perhaps infrequently employed in warfare. According to

Yate, "There were formerly, various kinds of offensive weapons, adapted to various kinds of warfare...most of which have been superceded by the introduction of the musket and the hatchet" (1835: 126).

CATALOGUE NO. 37

STILT STEP

POLYNESIA, MARQUESAS ISLANDS

LATE 18TH- EARLY 19TH CENTURY   E3327

WOOD 41.91 X 7 X 10.6 CM

BROWN UNIVERSITY, PROBABLY FROM

THE JENKS MUSEUM

Races, dances, and sporting events including competitions on stilts, *toko*, were popular activities among Eastern Polynesian youth. The distinctive, figural-carved stilt steps or footrests, collected as curiosities by early visitors to the Marquesas Islands, are unique to that island group. Each of a pair of stilt steps was bound to one of the stilt poles with braided coconut fiber, passing around the apex of the wedge-shaped step and through the opening behind the support figure. The present example shows much wear and evidence of long use.

Stilt steps are composed of an upward curving platform and a triangular lower section carved with a single supporting figure. This example has a single mask-like face as an additional embellishment on the exterior of the upward curving footrest surface. Of roughly triangular form, the footrest and the incorporated support figure are covered with fine parallel-grooved chevron patterns, the hands and face of the figure and the face on the upper edge of the footrest being reserved.

Most of the figures on stilt steps are consistent with the classic Polynesian sculpture style, including stocky muscular thighs and trunk, and broad facial features with large eyes, broad nose, and prominent lips. Tattoo, the prerogative of privileged classes of Polynesian society, is almost always represented on the figures. In this case, quadrilateral patterns appear on each cheek.

Although the stilt steps were made in pairs, they were frequently separated from their poles and collected singly by visitors. Stilt poles were often over six feet in length and would have been difficult to transport. For images of other stilt steps, poles, and their method of attachment, see Von den Steinen (1969 [1928]: 115-36).

CATALOGUE NO. 38

BARKCLOTH *MASI BOLABOLA*

POLYNESIA, FIJI, CAKAUDROVE DISTRICT

19TH CENTURY   E3105

BARKCLOTH 624.84 X 63.5 CM

BY EXCHANGE FROM THE PEABODY MUSEUM

OF SALEM IN 1954

Fijian men, and sometimes women, wore wrapped sashes or bandoliers with finely decorated triangular and other geometric panels of design, like this example. The fabric was produced and decorated by women, using precisely cut stencils. The technique continues in parts of Fiji today, however, instead of banana or other leaves, x-ray film is now the preferred material for stencils (Neich and Pendergrast, 1998 [1997]: 97).

The production of delicate undecorated barkcloth had divine associations in Fiji and in most other Polynesian islands. Finely patterned barkcloth like this example had wider secular connotations and was favored by visitors, who were especially attracted to the contrasting black on white designs.

This long sash with its finely executed triangular geometric panels in black and red on beige is a specialty of the Cacaudrove area (Neich and Pendergrast, 1998 [1997]: 100, 110-11). The edges are solid but are painted with a mock fringe.

CATALOGUE NO. 39

BARKCLOTH CAPE *'AHU FARA*

POLYNESIA, TAHITI

CIRCA 1790S   E3537

BARKCLOTH WITH RED-BROWN AND YELLOW PIGMENT

162.5 X 113.75 CM

DONATED BY MR. AND MRS. WILLIAM FARNSWORTH, THOUGHT TO HAVE

BEEN COLLECTED BY CAPTAIN FREEMAN MAYBERRY.

This cape or shawl with its collage-overlaid rectangular center of dark (probably once red) color and its fern-printed edges, corresponds closely with three *'ahu fara* collected on William Bligh's second breadfruit expedition of 1791-93. The three cloths were collected by members of the expedition and each probably constituted a ceremonial *taio*, or friendship gift (D'Alleva, 1995: figs. 1, 3). Shawls of this form, and especially of this size, were probably created specifically for use as ceremonial gifts and rather than as garments *per se* (D'Alleva, 1995: 35-36). The process of *taio* gift friendship, which also included the exchanging of names, is well recorded by early visitors to central Polynesia (Williamson, 1924, vol. III: 156-57).

'Ahu fara of this general form appear only to have been made prior to extensive foreign contact. However, the use of dye-saturated plant material to print the delicate designs on the borders and surface, especially notable on

Catalogue No. 54, persisted into the early 19th century. Whether this type of decoration may have been influenced by trade cloth, observation of embroidered borders on visitors' costumes, or other factors is not clear (Kooijman 1972: 271-82).

The technique of overlaying the cloth with a second smaller rectangle of solid color is unusual. The red color, originally quite strong on this panel, undoubtedly relates to the divine red feather belts in the Society Islands and the red feather cloaks of Hawaii. The border probably was once bright yellow. The combination of red and yellow were the sacred colors of Polynesia (ibid.: 107).

Change and evolution on the artistic as well as the political scene was ongoing throughout Polynesia prior to the arrival of the Europeans. However, as D'Alleva indicates, styles in barkcloth decoration evolved rapidly in Tahiti with the advent of new relationships with outsiders and attendant technical capabilities.

The design of these cloths reflects a dynamic of change and continuity that characterized many aspects of 18th century Tahitian society. For example, at the same time that Tahitian titleholders like Tu (Pomare I) were using European guns and trade goods to expand their authority, the artists who made these pieces were experimenting with new techniques and motifs presented by European cloth and clothing (D'Alleva, 1995: 35-36).

This type and period of *'ahu fara* is extremely rare, with only three examples, including the present, known to the author. Larger shawls with overall decorations of leaf patterns like Catalogue No. 54, though scarce, are far more numerous.

CATALOGUE NO. 40

HEADREST *KALI LALONI* OR *KALI TOLONI*

POLYNESIA, TONGA OR FIJI

19TH CENTURY   E2549

BAMBOO, WOOD, COCONUT FIBER 76.2 X 17.78 X 19.05 CM

PROVIDENCE FRANKLIN SOCIETY

CATALOGUE NO. 41

HEADREST *KALI LALONI* OR *KALI TOLONI*

POLYNESIA, TONGA OR FIJI

LATE 18TH- EARLY 19TH CENTURY   E2548

WOOD, COCONUT FIBER 43.18 X 16.51 CM

PROVIDENCE FRANKLIN SOCIETY

Headrests were important personal accessories especially in Polynesia, because the belief in *mana* designated the head as the most highly charged part of the individual. Headrests like these, limited to chiefly use, were stipulated as a portion of the bride's wealth according to Dhyne (1999: 413). Not surprisingly these important objects came to be regarded as heirloom property (St. Cartmail, 1997: 53).

It is not clear precisely which Tongan name may be appropriate to each of these forms. Discriminating between the rectangular versus the round feet and legs, and the flattened versus the round "bench" appears to have engendered some confusion in terminology among scholars. In addition, headrests of virtually identical form to Catalogue No. 41 may be carved from a single piece of wood, rather than constructed of three composite elements like both the present examples. Dhyne, citing Child, seems to favor *kali laloni* for three-part headrests and *kali toloni* for monoxylous ones (1999: 412). St. Cartmail does not take this criterion into consideration, but gives *kali laloni* for headrests with flat benches and rectangular legs and feet and *kali toloni* for those with round elements (1997: 53-54).

Headrests like these examples are recorded as coming from both Tonga and Fiji. Captain James Cook, who did not visit Fiji, collected similar headrests in Tonga or the "Friendly Islands," as he called them (Kaeppler, 1978: 229). As there was much trade between the two groups, is it possible that a design or even an individual object may have originated one place and have been transported to another, as many items were between Tonga and Fiji. St. Cartmail points out the Tongan "*kali toloni*" or "*kali laloni*" were also widely produced in Fiji by Tongan canoe builders and other craftsmen who flourished there during 18th and 19th centuries (1997: 52-57).

Catalogue No. 40 is similar in form and technology to Catalogue No. 41, except for its feet and legs of rectangular section and its bench of bamboo. Catalogue No. 41 has a slender curving bench with medial ridge beneath. For a similar example, with round feet believed to be from Fiji, see Clunie (1986: cat. 69).

The use of bamboo for the cross bar or bench of Catalogue No. 41 may indicate a Fijian origin, as nearly all those believed to be of Tongan origin are constructed of hardwood. The *kali loa*, which has a bamboo cross member, is the exception however, being designed to accommodate multiple sleepers. In the absence of more precise data, attribution of either of the headrests remains speculative.

CATALOGUE NO. 42

EAR ORNAMENT *HA AKAI*

POLYNESIA, MARQUESAS ISLANDS

19TH CENTURY   E3122

SPERM WHALE TOOTH 10.80 X 7.78 CM

BROWN UNIVERSITY

This is an example of an unfinished Marquesan ear ornament. The projecting rectangular element would have been relief-carved with a *tiki* figure and the spur would have been perforated, to admit a peg to secure the wearer's ear lobe against the back of the ornament. For an unfinished ear ornament in the James Hooper collection and other finished examples, see Phelps (1976: cat.

408 and pl. 50). For a variety of completed ear ornaments see also Oldman (1943: pl. 113), Von den Steinen (1969 [1928]: 24), and Dodge (1939: pl. VII).

The Marquesan man portrayed by Hodges in the atlas to Cook's second voyage is wearing large ear ornaments of shell. (Jopien and Smith, 1985: pls. 2.105, 2.105a). Similar ornaments were also made of wood; both materials prefigured the use of the marine ivory that became so popular and highly valued in the 19th century (Von den Steinen (1969 [1928]: 25), (Lavondès, 1995: 32-33).

CATALOGUE NO. 43

BARKCLOTH *MASI* **OR** *SEYAVU*

POLYNESIA, FIJI

19TH CENTURY   E3499

BARKCLOTH 264.16 X 58.42 CM

HAFFENREFFER, 1955

This light, undecorated, thin-fringed textile has been hammered to a gauzy transparency. Composed of several lengths joined together with the fringes retained as ornamental bands of suspensions, this cloth was undoubtedly intended as a loincloth, turban, or sash for a chiefly individual.

In Fiji as in many other Polynesian Islands, the most sacred and highly valued barkcloth was undecorated white material, *seyavu*. Like this example, it was often processed to an extreme thinness. Such "linen" was worn close to the body as a loincloth, *malo*, turban, or scarf. It was used ceremonially to drape sacred objects and enclosures. Pieces of thin barkcloth as large as 10 by 30 meters are also recorded having been used for mosquito netting (Kooijman, 1972: 410; Clunie, 1986: 127).

Large amounts of *seyavu* were involved in inter-tribal presentations. On such occasions, the visiting dignitary or chief might wear the entire quantity of the prospective gift, carefully wrapped in billowing folds about his person. He would then disrobe, as it were, and present the gift to the chiefly host, who would accept and distribute it among his followers. Some of these ceremonial "robes" were in excess of 100 meters in length. Kooijman, citing Kleinschmidt, reproduces a drawing of a chief with a strip of *masi* "about 180 meters hung on his body" at a presentation to the governor of Fiji in 1877 (1972: 412, fig. 436). Kaeppler reports that similar ceremonial presentations of barkcloth continue in Tahiti even into the 21st century (2002).

CATALOGUE NO. 44

THROWING CLUB *I ULA TAVATAVA*

POLYNESIA, FIJI

EARLY 19TH CENTURY   E2737

WOOD 41.28 X 9.53 CM

PROVIDENCE FRANKLIN SOCIETY

CATALOGUE NO. 45

THROWING CLUB *I ULA TAVATAVA*

POLYNESIA, FIJI

19TH CENTURY   E2269

WOOD 45.09 X 12.07 CM

PROVIDENCE FRANKLIN SOCIETY

CATALOGUE NO. 46

THROWING CLUB *I ULA TAVATAVA*

POLYNESIA, FIJI

19TH CENTURY   E2736A

WOOD 40.64 X 10.16 CM

PROVIDENCE FRANKLIN SOCIETY

CATALOGUE NO. 47

THROWING CLUB WITH IVORY INLAY *KOLO* OR *ULA*

POLYNESIA, TONGA OR FIJI

19TH CENTURY   E2286

WOOD, MARINE (PROBABLY WHALE) IVORY

46.67 X 10.8 CM

PROVIDENCE FRANKLIN SOCIETY

CATALOGUE NO. 48

ROUND HEADED THROWING CLUB *I ULA DRISIA*

POLYNESIA, FIJI

EARLY 19TH CENTURY   E2668

WOOD (WITH SECONDARY IRON SCREW FRAGMENT)

41.5 X 9 CM

PROVIDENCE FRANKLIN SOCIETY

Throwing clubs were ubiquitous in Fijian warfare. They were among the most feared weapon of the Fijian arsenal, as they were thrown considerable distances with much accuracy and were often lethal. Throwing clubs were also employed as hand clubs and used to dispatch wounded adversaries. For a full variety of forms and terms see Clunie (1977: 59-63 and fig. 21) and Ewins (1982: 26-27).

Fijian throwing clubs varied in their degree of elaboration. Clubs that consisted of mere root masses with sapling handles were only slightly trimmed and smoothed. Simple round headed examples, *i ula drisia*, like Catalogue No. 48, might have had human molars fixed in the naturally-occurring cavi-

ties of the rounded-off head. Finely lobed or gadroon-carved *i ula tavatava* like Catalogue Nos. 44-46 are good examples of the most finished type of *ula*. Catalogue No. 44 is the most finely carved throwing club in the collection, with double rows of fluting around the head.

The *kolo* or *ula*, Catalogue No. 47, is especially rare. The presence of the ivory inlays indicates that this club would undoubtedly have belonged to an important chiefly individual. Some of the ivory pieces have openwork with wood reserved in the shape of four-pointed stars. The method of carving the root mass, clipping the roots in symmetrical fashion, is also an unusual technique to be found on throwing clubs.

Tonga, where sperm whales frequently stranded, was the pre-contact source of ivory for the Fiji Islands and Tongan ivory workmanship is well documented. Mariner states in his observations around 1805, "This kind of ivory they also use to inlay their clubs as well as their wooden pillows" (Martin, 1827, vol. I: 250-51).

St. Cartmail mentions the inlaid throwing club, *kolo* in connection with the Tongan arsenal (1997: 126-27, Fig. 80.) For a fine Fijian *ula* with ivory inlay, see also Clunie (1986: 102-03, fig. 124, 5.) and Clunie (1977: 59-62).

CATALOGUE NO. 49

CLUB *SALI*

POLYNESIA, FIJI

LATE 18TH- EARLY 19TH CENTURY   E2289

WOOD, SHELL, COCONUT FIBER 106.68 X 22.86 CM

PROVIDENCE FRANKLIN SOCIETY

This fine old *sali*, a curving spurred club with carved faces, is especially notable for its fully shell bead-wrapped handle and coconut fiber-wrapped grip. The *sali* takes its name from its resemblance to "the clawed flower of one of the wild banana-like plants (*Musa* species) that grow in the Fiji bush" (Clunie, 1977: 54). The utility of the opposing spur-shaped extension on this form is unclear, however the beveled and curving blade was designed to "cut through and snap bone rather than smash it" (ibid.). For a similar club, without the shell decoration, collected in the first quarter of the 19th century, see Endicott (1923: fig 1).

The presence of the discoidal shell beads on this example is very rare. The coconut fiber through which they are strung is meticulously attached to the club handle itself by small loops of sennit which are stitched through double perforations in the actual wood surface. This technique serves to support the coils, which would otherwise have a tendency to slide along the handle according to the dictates of gravity or inertia.

A similarly decorated *sali* is illustrated by Clunie (1977: fig 3-g), although he does not mention whether or not the club handle is perforated for supportive stitching of the coconut fiber shell bindings. The possible signifi-cance of this elaborate and very laborious decoration is uncertain. It seems likely that this object may have been accorded a high status in its own right, possibly on account of its having been used in an important victory or uti-lized in a specific killing.

Clunie points out the similarity of such shell disks to Melanesian shell cur-rency strands (1977: 54). For examples of comparable shell beads on curren-cy belts and necklaces from Kiribati, see Treide (1997: cats. 168, 9). Similar shell disk beads appear on the Fijian spear, *gadregadre*, Catalogue No. 17. It is possible that the use of shell beads like these examples died out with the availability of glass beads which were extensively used by foreign traders in the early 19th century (Endicott, 1923: 18, 7).

CATALOGUE NO. 50

BARKCLOTH *SIAPO MAMANU*

POLYNESIA, SAMOA,

FIRST QUARTER 20TH CENTURY   E3492

BARKCLOTH, BLACK AND YELLOW PIGMENT

175.26 X 144.8 CM

HAFFENREFFER MUSEUM, 1955

This rectangular, freehand-painted barkcloth, *siapo mamanu*, has overall leaf designs in black, *pani*, and yellow, *ango*, and a border of triangles and hatched lines. For a discussion of the traditional method of painting *siapo*, using pandanus fruit "keys" for brushes, and other naturally occurring mate-rials, see Hiroa (1971 [1930]: 306-07).

Pritchard relates how the women of Leone, where there was a thriving cot-tage industry in the production of *siapo* for export up until WWII, derived their inspiration for new designs and additional colors from the stained glass windows of the church there (1984:15). *Siapo mamanu* like the present exam-ple were common productions for this trade during the early 20th century (ibid.: 12-21). See Neich and Pendergrast for a similar design on a round *siapo*, from American Samoa, also made for the tourist market (1997: 30).

CATALOGUE NO. 51

FAN

POLYNESIA, COOK ISLANDS, PROBABLY

RAROTONGA

19TH CENTURY   E3355

WOOD, PANDANUS LEAF, COCONUT FIBER

36.58 X 29.21 CM

DONATED BY GRACE ABBOT FLETCHER IN 1955, AND POSSIBLY COLLECTED BY HER GRANDFATHER, JOEL ABBOT, WHO WAS CAPTAIN OF THE FRIGATE *MACEDONIAN*, WHICH SAILED WITH PERRY TO JAPAN IN 1853

Plaited fans are common throughout Polynesia. The shapes vary regionally from group to group. Polynesian fans with carved wooden handles are rela-tively rare. The design of the present example is specific to Rarotonga, "with two heads back to back, and the eye and mouth forms peculiar to the carving on that island" (Hiroa, 1944: 59). For a related motif from a god figure in the British Museum see Hiroa, (1944: fig. 229).

The fan's plaited "screen" has a centrally placed sleeve to accept the taper-ing wooden handle. Carved with an abstract Janus figure, this handle was undoubtedly the property of a chiefly individual (Phelps, 1976: 130). It was probably used with many disposable plaited screens like the present one. Some Rarotongan fan handles are more elaborately carved and display more clearly distinguishable anthropomorphic figures. See Idiens (1990: 31-32); Barrow (1979: pl. 81); Barrow (1973: pl. 215); and Mack (1982: 234-35).

CATALOGUE NO. 52

CLUB *KINIKINI*

POLYNESIA, FIJI

LATE 18TH- EARLY 19TH CENTURY   E2300

WOOD, PIGMENT 118.11 X 31.12 CM

BROWN UNIVERSITY

This broad, thin, paddle-shaped club has a blade surface decorated with fine, hatched designs; there is a "v"-shaped cross bar and a medial rib on either side. The lower quadrants are decorated with pinwheel or floral designs which have orange-pigmented centers. The round handle terminates in an expanded butt. This example is one of the finest and earliest known to the writer. The presence of the pigment and the evident early technology used to craft it indicates that it was probably carved before the widespread availability of iron tools.

According to Clunie, priests and high chiefs carried this type of club as an insignia of rank. In battle, the club might have served as a cutting weapon and also as a shield against arrows and other projectiles like the *culacula* (1977: 56).

The man who carried such a club was esteemed not only by his allies, but also would have been eagerly sought out by his enemies. Relatively few men were entitled to carry the *kinikini* and owing to their broad, thin construction they were subject to being damaged. They were phased out of the arsenal early in the 19th century, for with the widespread use of firearms, he who carried a kinikini in battle would have been a marked man. This club type is rare in collections. The present example is in a remarkable state of preservation, considering that it may be over 200 years old. For other examples of *kinikini*, see Clunie (1977: fig. 8, a-b) and Ewins (1982 cat. m 4919).

CATALOGUE NO. 53

CLUB *CULACULA*

POLYNESIA FIJI

EARLY 19TH CENTURY   E2525

WOOD 102.24 X 15.24 CM

PROVIDENCE FRANKLIN SOCIETY

The *culacula* is characterized by a paddle-shaped blade with serrated edges, a pronounced cross bar and an expanded butt flange. According to Clunie this form originated in Samoa or Tonga where, indeed, spatulate and paddle-bladed clubs are more common. Like the *kinikini*, Catalogue No. 52, the *culacula* was used as a cutting and slicing weapon as well serving to shield its owner from missiles (1977: 55, fig.7C); see also Ewins (1982: 44-45).

The present example is smooth in its contours and the butt, in typical Fijian style, has no lug, but a slightly expanded terminus. Clunie states that this form was popular in the coastal regions of Fiji (1977: 55).

CATALOGUE NO. 54

SHAWL OR CLOAK *AHUFARA*

POLYNESIA, TAHITI

CIRCA 1800-1820   E3282

BARKCLOTH WITH RED-BROWN AND TRACES OF

YELLOW PIGMENT 232.41 X 165.1 CM

RECEIVED FROM BROWN UNIVERSITY WITH MATERIAL

FROM THE JENKS MUSEUM

This barkcloth is of beige color with brown leaf-printed patterns distributed sparsely across the surface and placed in triangles at the corners. At one time the color of the patterning was undoubtedly of a stronger reddish hue and the background may have been of an overall yellow tone produced by the use of turmeric. Kooijman suggests that Tahitians were inspired to develop this decorative style in response to florally decorated cloth brought to the islands by European visitors in the late 18th century (1972: 21). D'Alleva notes however, that William Bligh's Bounty journal of 1777-78 mentions barkcloth decoration using leaf impressions to produce "the prettiest" designs. Scant trade cloth could have reached Tahiti by this date and she therefore concludes that not only the technique but also its use would seem to predate widespread foreign contacts (1995: 33). Catalogue No. 39 is also an example of this technique of decoration on barkcloth from the early contact period.

Neich and Prendergrast outline the manufacturing process which first involved men who harvested the bark; women then took over the process, first working in or at the edge of streams to soak and separate the inner bark and leaving it to dry in sheets. (1998 [1997]: 85-86). A large gathering of women would be involved in the process of beating this intermediate cloth into thin tissue, working in district-based groups (D'Alleva: 2002). Ellis describes such a gathering:

In the manufacture of cloth, the females of all ranks were employed; and the queen, and wives of the chiefs of the highest rank, strove to excel in some department—in the elegance of pattern, or the brilliancy of the colour. They are fond of society, and worked in large parties, in open and temporary houses erected for the purpose. Visiting one of these houses at Eimeo, I saw sixteen or twenty females all employed. The queen sat in the midst, surrounded by several chief women, each with a mallet in her hand, beating the bark that was spread before her. The queen worked as diligently and cheerfully as any present. (1831: vol. I. 184).

Ellis further notes, that the plain barkcloth used in religious rites was made by men (1831: 186). For illustrations of other Tahitian barkcloth decorated with impressions of plant material, see Barrow (1979:29, pl. 30-31); D'Alleva (1998: cat. 89); D'Alleva (1995: figs. 1, 3); and Kooijman (1972: 21-26, figs. 8-9, 10; 2, 1).

CATALOGUE NO. 55

SCOOP OR LADLE

POLYNESIA, AUSTRAL ISLANDS, RA'IVAVAE

EARLY 19TH CENTURY   E2290

WOOD 112.4 X 9.525 CM

DONATED TO THE PROVIDENCE FRANKLIN

SOCIETY BY CAPTAIN PETER F. EVERS

This object, consisting of an oval bowl with a long projecting handle and a carved conical pommel, though rare, compares with several other known examples. All seem to have been a post contact period elaboration of earlier elliptical bowls, similarly carved around their rims but without handles. For examples of bowls with and without handles, cf. Hall (1921: figs. 65-66) and Barrow (1979, 54-68).

Information about the use of such bowls is not available. Hall suggests a possible ritual function for the handled bowls, hypothesizing that they may have been used by attendants to feed taboo individuals or to make offerings to deities (1921a: 192-93).

Priest's dishes with handles in Fiji, and feeding funnels among the Maori, were used to safeguard individuals from contamination in this way. There are no indications that such practices occurred among the Austral Islanders, however. It seems fitting, as Mack suggests, that they be classified with the carved paddles, such as Catalogue Nos. 5, 6, and 7, as items fashioned for tourists and traders (1982: 220).

CATALOGUE NO. 56

TROLLING LURE FOR BONITO *PA HI AKU*

POLYNESIA, HAWAII

19TH CENTURY   E3123A

SHELL, HUMAN BONE, *OLANA* FIBER,

BOAR BRISTLE 11.43 X 1.91 CM

BROWN UNIVERSITY

CATALOGUE NO. 57

TROLLING LURE FOR BONITO *PAATU*

POLYNESIA, SAMOA

19TH CENTURY   E2304

SHELL, TORTOISE SHELL, COCONUT FIBER,

REMAINS OF BOAR BRISTLE HACKLE

5.40 X 1.91 CM

DONOR UNRECORDED

CATALOGUE NO. 58

TROLLING LURE FOR BONITO *PAATU*

POLYNESIA, SAMOA

19TH CENTURY   E2313

SHELL, TURTLE SHELL, COCONUT AND OTHER

FIBER 4.45 X 1.62 CM,

BROWN UNIVERSITY

CATALOGUE NO. 59

FISH HOOK AND SNOOD

POLYNESIA, TAHITI

19TH CENTURY   E3124

SHELL, FIBER 6.35 X 4.45 CM

BROWN UNIVERSITY

According to Hiroa, the traditional material used in the Hawaiian bonito hook was *olana* fiber, a platform of pearl shell, *pa* or *uhi*, and usually a human bone point, *lala* (1964 [1957]: 333-35). Concerning the use of human bone he writes:

Hawaiians believed that fishooks made from the bones of people without hair on their bodies, who were termed olohe, were more attractive to fish than hooks from normal bones. Thus the olohe individuals ran the risk of being prematurely dispatched to supply the luck-bringing material (1964 [1957]: 325).

Catalogue No. 56, a composite trolling lure, is a typical example of the traditional Hawaiian bonito fishing lure, *pa hi aku*. Bonito fishing throughout the Pacific islands is done by trolling such lures from a moving boat through groups of bonito who are caught in the act of pursuing schools of small of fish. This activity is exciting and requires dexterity and skill. The hooks themselves are not barbed to facilitate disengaging them from the caught fish and to enable the angler to recast quickly, taking advantage of what is usually an opportunity of very limited duration (Hiroa, 1964 [1957]: 337-38). See also Beasley (1980 [1928]: 52-53, pl. LXXXVII).

Catalogue Nos. 57 and 58 are small trolling lures also for bonito. The turtle shell hook is lashed to the pearl shell platform and each retains its bundled leader or snood as it would have been carried in a tackle box ready for unwinding and use on board. In Samoa in 1930 Hiroa observed, "*pa atu* were still in common use...made and lashed with the old techniques except for the implements used" (1971 [1930]: 497-98). Concerning the manufacture of fish hooks he writes:

The making of hooks was expert work and a master fisherman (tautai) was not always a good hook maker. A certain amount of ceremonial is observed in making bonito hooks. The craftsman works indoors seated on a raised pile of mats. When employed by a chief, the chief has to make a special oven of food and send him a basket of cooked food of good quality. (Hiroa, 1971 [1030]: 495).

For a drawing of a craftsman in a cross-legged posture binding a *pa atu*, see Hiroa (1971 [1930]: fig. 286).

Catalogue No. 59 is an elegantly formed bait hook with its original snood in excellent condition. For similar examples see Beasley, (1980 [1928], pls. LV, LVIII, LXI).

CATALOGUE NO. 60
FORK
POLYNESIA, FIJI
EARLY 19TH CENTURY   E3523
WOOD
BISHOP MUSEUM VIA EXCHANGE IN 1956

In several parts of Polynesia, ritual bowls and other feeding implements were devised to safeguard attendants of chiefly individuals who were frequently subject to taboos and restrictions involving the consumption of food and other bodily functions.

In certain cases, individuals were not allowed to touch food with their hands. They might also cause harm to those whom they touched or who chanced to touch them. Long-handled feeding dishes, feeding funnels, and so-called "cannibal forks" were employed in various ways to facilitate this system of practice.

In Fiji, the hands and lips of priests and high chiefs were *tabou*, and were not allowed to touch the food they ate; their wives or attendants customarily fed them. A feast of human flesh usually took place in the sacred temple, however, a place from which women and lesser individuals were restricted. For such occasions so-called "cannibal forks" were employed so that these privileged individuals might feed themselves without touching the human flesh. For a thorough discussion of cannibalism and related practices in Fiji, see Clunie (1977: 35-42) and Clunie (1986: 120, cat. 204).

CATALOGUE NO. 61
BOWL *TANO'A*
POLYNESIA, TONGA
19TH CENTURY   E3097
WOOD, COCONUT FIBER 67.95 X 17.78 CM
PRESENTED TO THE FRANKLIN SOCIETY
JUNE 1, 1841 BY CAPTAIN NATHANIEL W. SOULE OF THE WHALESHIP *BOWDITCH*: NOTATION STATES THAT THE BOWL WAS "PURCHASED FROM CHIEF JOSIAH AT VA VOU [SIC], TONGA".

This large four-legged vessel of abstract zoomorphic form has a shallow conical bowl with an everted rim, the interior with *kava* residues and some flaking. The perforated lug, *taunga*, which may be read as an abstract head, retains a frayed original length of braided coconut fiber suspension cord.

Kava is the drink of the gods, first introduced to earth by the god Tangaloa, according to Polynesian myth (Williamson, 1939: 101-02). Prepared from the shredded or masticated root of a pepper tree, *Piper methysticum*, it is a mild narcotic. The consumption of *kava* often accompanies priestly ritual and in some islands was limited to religious observances.

Kava drinking, prevalent in central Polynesia, is most thoroughly documented in the cultures of Fiji, Samoa, and Tonga. The social drinking of *kava* in these three island groups probably developed from the *kava* circle of Tu'i Tonga, the king, in the 18th century. Elaborate social protocols and conventions for preparing and serving the beverage, especially related to the chiefly rank of the participants, evolved during this period and spread to neighboring Fiji (St. Cartmail, 1997: 68-69).

In Tonga, *kava* was drunk privately at home, in larger social gatherings, on occasions of state, as well as for religious ceremonies. Normally the highest ranking individual, usually a chief or the king, would preside at public *kava* drinking ceremonies which were usually limited to male participants. In the case of a religious ritual, in which a god was to be summoned and consulted, his inspired priest would take the place of the high chief. Out of deference for the anticipated presence of the god, the chief would take an inferior position in the circle.

The traditional Tongan *kava* circle was essentially of oval configuration, with the most exalted individuals concentrated at the upper two-thirds of its circumference. The highest ranking chief took his place in the highest or most central position in this "superior circle" as it was called. The *tano'a*, the *kava* and the preparators occupied a position in the center of the "inferior circle" which was actually the lower third of the *kava* circle proper. Lesser chiefs and officials would be seated in the "inferior circle." Attendants, sons and daughters of chiefs, and others would sit in an exterior circle, actually comprised of succeeding rows of the "inferior circle," according to Mariner and other early witnesses as cited by Williamson (1939: 72-73).

James Cook observed and was a guest at *kava* drinking ceremonies on Tonga during his second voyage of exploration, 1772-75 (St. Cartmail, 1997: 68-70). The *tano'a* Cook collected are not unlike Catalogue No. 61; compare (Kaeppler, 1998: 19, 20 and 1978: 226-27).

Kava bowls are common in Western collections, however Catalogue No. 61 is a particularly good example, retaining its suspension cord and evidence of long use when it was acquired by Captain Soule in 1841. The survival of its collection history is of particular importance.

CATALOGUE NO. 62
BARKCLOTH *KAPA*
POLYNESIA, HAWAIIAN ISLANDS
EARLY 19TH CENTURY   E3566
BARKCLOTH, PIGMENT 325.12 X 238.8 CM
DONATED BY DR. GEORGE E. MCCLELLAND
ACCOMPANIED BY THE WRITTEN NOTATION: "TO MRS.
WADSWORTH HARBARD(?) FROM MRS. BINGHAM."

The repeating designs on this fine Hawaiian barkcloth, *kapa*, are meticulously composed of smaller units produced by a sequence of block printed geometric elements from bamboo stamps, *ohe kapala*. The printing of delicate design elements using *ohe kapala* was an early contact development as previously noted with text for Catalogue Nos. 28 and 29.

The overall design of this unusual *kapa* is based on those found on East Indian paisley textiles. The central field contains rows of diagonal printed elements and three borders of pinwheels, *botehs*, and overlapping roundels. This constitutes a rare example of a native Hawaiian artist's evidently taking her inspiration from a very specific design on imported material. The borrowing of the paisley design is thus unique, in the opinion of the author.

The provenance of this object is also significant. Reverend Hiram Bingham and his wife Sybil (presumably the Mrs. Bingham from whom the donor received this *kapa*) sailed with the first American missionaries to the Hawaiian Islands in 1919. Their ministry in Honolulu lasted 21 years. Sybil (*ne*. Moseley) was born in 1792 in Westfield, and died in Easthampton, Massachusetts in 1848 (Hawaiian Mission Children's Society, 1937 [1901]: 7, 35-37).

The making and decorating of *kapa* was women's work and might have been parallel with needlework and other occupations in which women participated while convening faith-based groups. Whether Mrs. Bingham may have been present during the decoration or perhaps even possessed the shawl that inspired the design of this unique cross-cultural product will probably never be known. The circumstances surrounding its creation are nonetheless intriguing.

CATALOGUE NO. 63

CLUB

POLYNESIA, TONGA

19TH CENTURY   E2524

WOOD 96.52 X 9.53 CM

PROVIDENCE FRANKLIN SOCIETY

This paddle-shaped club with raised flange at the intersection of its blade has an oval handle that gradually becomes square in section toward the butt. The butt terminus is cut flat and has no perforation. The club surface is covered overall with zigzag carving that recalls barkcloth or tattoo patterns. Both Hiroa and St. Cartmail have problems with the attribution of this type of club vacillating between Tonga and Samoa respectively (1971[1930]: 598-99) and (1997: 132-33).

CATALOGUE NO. 64

CLUB *BOWAI*

POLYNESIA, FIJI

19TH CENTURY   E2547

WOOD 91.44 X 7.94 CM

PROVIDENCE FRANKLIN SOCIETY

The typical Fijian *bowai* is a baton-shaped club, only the grip of which is usually carved. The overall decoration of this example may be an indication of Tongan influence, a cultural factor strongly felt in Fiji from the beginning of the 18th century, according to St. Cartmail (1997: 68-70). As has been noted in the discussion of the headrests, Catalogue Nos. 40 and 41, this cross-cultural art style is interesting from an historic and cultural perspective, but is by no means rare. For the incidence of Tongan design among 19th century Fijian clubs see Clunie (1986: 184, cat. 184). See also Clunie (1977: fig. 10).

CATALOGUE NO. 65

CLUB *MOUNGALAULAU*

POLYNESIA, TONGA

18TH-19TH CENTURY   E3114

WOOD 109.2 X 10.8 CM

BROWN UNIVERSITY

Although Tongan clubs are frequently distinguished by richly carved surfaces, this rare example is also embellished with figural elements interspersed among panels of zigzag, notched, and ridged elements. Five human figures in athletic postures wield clubs and carry containers of plants, possibly *kava*. There are also figures of turtles and an unidentified quadruped.

The butt of the club has a convex lug for the attachment of a wrist cord, which is a common Tongan feature. Cords were useful to suspend the weapon when it was not in use and also to secure the fighter's grip. This would have been especially crucial when the weapon and the fighter's hands might be covered with the blood of combat.

Clubs were carried as an insignia of rank, for self-defense, and also for offense in times other than outright war. Chiefs had the power of life and death over their subjects and capitol punishment was commonplace. A chief might resort to "club law" whenever he was moved to do so. Williamson quotes Lawry's account of 1850:

A chief dealt death to whom he would with the end of his club, and a man who was found refractory was quickly dispatched (1924, vol. III: 118).

This club was certainly the property of a chief. The human elements may refer to the owner's progenitors. The images of turtles have special significance because the turtle was regarded as an animal of divine origin whose flesh was restricted to gods and near divine mortals, namely chiefs (Williamson, 1924, vol. II, 245-55, 311).

For several examples of *moungalaulau*, see Oldman (1943: pls. 49-510 and 50-510) and St. Cartmail (1997: 138-41). Clubs like this might have been ceremonial presents. They were also traded to foreigners. For examples collected on voyages of James Cook, see Kaeppler (1978: 238-40).

ALEXANDER, JAMES EDWIN [MAJOR-GENERAL SIR]

1873   *Bush Fighting: Illustrated by Remarkable Actions and Incidents of the Maori War in New Zealand*, London: Sampson Low, Marston, Low and Searle.

ATTENBOROUGH, DAVID

1990   "The First Figures to be Collected from Easter Island," *Courier Forschung-Institut Senckenberg*, 125: 40-50.

BARROW, TERENCE

1979   *The Art of Tahiti and the Neighboring Society, Cook and Austral Islands*, London: Thames & Hudson.

1973   *Art and Life in Polynesia*, Rutland and Tokyo: Charles E. Tuttle Company, Inc.

1969   *Maori Wood Sculpture of New Zealand*, Rutland and Tokyo: Charles E. Tuttle.

BEASLEY, HARRY G.

1980 [1928]   *Pacific Island Records Fish Hooks*, facsimile reprint, London: John Hewett.

BERAN, HARRY

1988   *Betel-chewing Equipment of East New Guinea*, Aylesbury: Shire Publications, Ltd.

1980   *An Exhibition of Art of the Massim Region of Papua New Guinea from the Collections in New South Wales and Canberra*, Wollongong: Wollongong City Gallery.

BLACKBURN, MARK

1999   *Tattoos from Paradise*, Atglen: Schiffer Publishing Ltd.

BRIGHAM, WILLIAM T.

1911   "*Ka Hana Kapa*," *The Making of Bark-Cloth in Hawaii*, Memoirs of the Bernice Pauahi Bishop Museum of Polynesian Ethnology and Natural History, volume III, Honolulu: Bishop Museum Press.

1906   *Old Hawaiian Carvings*, Memoirs of the Bernice Pauahi Bishop Museum of Polynesian Ethnology and Natural History, volume II, No. 2 , Honolulu: Bishop Museum Press.

BURROWS, EDWIN G.

1936   *Ethnology of Futuna*, Bernice P. Bishop Museum Bulletin, Honolulu: Bishop Museum.

CHAUVET, STEPHEN

1934   *L'ile de Paques et ses Mystères*, Paris: Aux Editions "Tel".

CLUNIE, FURGUS

1977   *Fijian Weapons and Warefare*, Bulletin no. 2. Suva: Fiji Museum.

1986   *Yalo I Viti, Shades of Viti: A Fiji Museum Catalogue*. Suva: Fiji Museum.

COWAN, JAMES

1910   *The Maoris of New Zealand*, Christchurch, Wellington and Dunedin; Melbourne and London: Whitcombe & Tombs Limited.

COX, J. HALLEY AND WILLIAM H. DAVENPORT

1988   *Hawaiian Sculpture: Revised Edition*, Honolulu: University of Hawaii Press.

D'ALLEVA, ANNE (ADALLEVA@COMPUSERVE.COM)

2002   Re: "Catalogue texts for your inspection and advice," Email to Norman Hurst (Nhurst@compuserve.com). April 30.

D'ALLEVA, ANNE

1998   *Arts of the Pacific Islands*, New York, Harry N Abrams, Inc., Publishers

1996   Unpublished manuscript pages 2-4.

1995   "Change and Continuity in Decorated Tahitian Barkcloth from Bligh's Second Breadfruit Voyage, 1791-1793," *Pacific Arts*, Nos. 11 & 12, July 1995, 29-42, Pacific Arts Association.

1990   *Art and Artifacts of Polynesia*, Cambridge: Hurst Gallery.

D'ALLEVA, ANNE AND NORMAN HURST

1987   *Art of Polynesia*, Cambridge: Hurst Gallery.

DHYNE, JEFFREY

1999   "Tongan Headrests: Notes on Terminology and Function," *The Journal of the Polynesian Society*, vol. 108, No. 4, December, 1999, 411-16.

DODGE, ERNEST STANLEY

1939   *The Marquesas Islands Collection in the Peabody Museum of Salem*, Salem: Peabody Museum.

DONNE, T. E.

1927   *The Maori Past and Present: An Account of a Highly Attractive, Intelligent People, their Doubtful Origin, Their Customs & Ways of Living, Art, Methods of Warfare, Hunting & Other Characteristics Mental & Physical*, London: Seeley Service & Co., Limited.

EILERS, DR. ANNELIESE

1934   *Inseln Um Ponape. Kapamarangi, Nukuor, Ngatik, Mokil, Pingelap. Ergebnisse der Südsee-Expedition 1908-1910*, Dr. G. Thilenius, ed., II Ethnographie: Band 8, Hamburg: Friederichsen, De Gruyter & Co. m.b.h.

ELLIS, WILLIAM

1831   *Polynesian Researches*, London: Fisher, Son & Jackson

ENDICOTT, WILLIAM

1923   *Wrecked among Cannibals in the Fijis: A Narrative of Shipwreck and Adventure in the South Seas*, Salem: Marine Research Society.

ESEN-BAUER, HEIDE-MARGARET

1989   *1500 Jahre Kultur der Osterinsel: Schatz aus dem Land des Hotu Matua*, Mainz am Rhein: Verlag Philipp von Zabern.

EWENS, ROD

1982   *Fijian Artifacts: The Tasmanian Museum and Art Gallery Collection*, Hobart: The Tasmanian Museum and Art Gallery.

FELDMAN, JEROME AND DAVID HANLON (JFELDMAN@HPU.EDU)

2002   "Re: Gbaloali" Email to Norman Hurst (Nhurst@compuserve.com). March 7.

FELDMAN, JEROME

1984   "Form and Function in the Art of Micronesia," in Feldman, Jerome and Rubenstein, Donald H., eds., *The Art of Micronesia*, pp. 15-23, Honolulu: The University of Hawaii.

FORCE, ROLAND W. AND MARYANNE FORCE

1971   *The Fuller Collection of Pacific Artifacts*, New York, Washington: Praeger Publishers.

HALL, HENRY USHER

1921a   "Woodcarvings of the Austral Islands," in The Museum Journal vol. 12 No. 3, Philadelphia: The University Museum, University of Pennsylvania, pp. 179-99.

1921b   "Art of the Marquesas Islanders," *The Museum Journal* vol. 12 No. 4, Philadelphia: The University Museum, University of Pennsylvania, pp. 252-92.

HAUSER-SCHÄUBLIN, BIRGITTA

1998   "Marquesas–Plagued by Misfortune" 221-233 and 324-325 in *James Cook: Gifts and Treasures from the South Seas/Gaben und Schätze aus der Südsee*, Hauser-Schäublin, Birgitta and and Krüger, Gundolf, eds. Munchen and New York: Prestel Verlag.

HAWAIIAN MISSION CHILDREN'S SOCIETY (NO AUTHOR GIVEN)

1937 [1901]   *Missionary Album*, Honolulu: Hawaiian Mission Children's Society.

HEERMANN, INGRID AND MENTER, ULRICH

1990   *Schmuck der Südsee*, München: Prestel Verlag.

HEYERDAHL, THOR

1975   *The Art of Easter Island*, New York: Doubleday & Company, Inc.

HIROA, TE RANGI (SIR PETER H. BUCK)

1964 [1957]   *Arts and Crafts of Hawaii*. Bernice P. Bishop Museum, Special Publication 45, Honolulu: Bishop Museum Press.

1944   *Arts and Crafts of the Cook Islands*. Bernice P. Bishop Museum, Bulletin 179, Honolulu: Bishop Museum Press.

1971 [1930]   *Samoan Material Culture*, Bernice P. Bishop Museum Bulletin 75, New York: Kraus Reprint Co.

HURST, NORMAN

2001   "From Cellar to Spotlight: Three Previously Unpublished Easter Island Sculptures from the Providence Museum of Natural History and Planetarium." Pages 321-329. In: *Pacific 2000, Proceedings of the Fifth International Congress on Easter Island and the Pacific*. Ed. Christopher M. Stevenson, Georgia Lee and Frank J. Morin. The Easter Island Foundation, 2001.

1997   *Power and Prestige: Arts of Island Melanesia and the Polynesian Outliers*. Cambridge: Hurst Gallery.

IDIENS, DALE

1900   *Cook Islands Art*, Princes Risborough: Shire Publications Ltd.

JENKINS, IRVING

1989   *The Hawaiian Calabash*, Honolulu: Editions Limited

JOHNSON, RUBELLITE KINNEY

1997   Unpublished manuscript for Abigail K. Kawananakoa Foundation, Honolulu, to Tracey K. Brussat, Director, Museum of Natural History.

JOPIEN, RÜDIGER AND BERNARD SMITH

1985   *The Art of Captain Cook's Voyages, Volume Two the Voyage of the Resolution and Adventure*, New Haven and London: Yale University Press

KANE, HERB KAWAINUI

1996   Letter to the author. December, 11.

KAEPPLER, ADRIENNE L.

2002   "Exploring the Designs and Uses of Tapa in Polynesia." Opening Lecture *Embedded Nature: Tapa Cloths from the Pacific Islands*. The Peabody Museum, Harvard University. Haller Hall, Cambridge. March, 6.

"Rapa Nui Art and Aesthetics" 32-41 in *Splendid Isolation: Art of Easter Island*, Kjellgren, Eric, New York, The Metropolitan Museum of Art.

1998   *From the Stone Age to the Space Age in 200 Years: Tongan Art and Society on the Eve of the Millennium*, Nuku'alofa: The Tongan National Museum.

1978   *"Artificial Curiosities:" being an Exposition of Native Manufactures Collected on the Three Pacific Voyages of Captain Jame S. Cook, R. N.*, Bishop Museum Special Publication 65, Honolulu: Bishop Museum Press.

KATO, RIOKU

1997   *Micronesia–Navigators and Their Culture*, Ota: Folk Museum of Ota City.

KEATE, GEORGE

1789   *An Account of the Pelew Islands, situated in the Western Part of the Pacific Ocean. Composed from the Journals and Communications of Captain Henry Wilson, and Some of his Officers, Who, in August 1783, Were There Shipwrecked in The Antelope, Packet Belonging to the Honourable East India Company*, London: Printed for Captain Wilson.

KJELLGREN, ERIC

2001   *Splendid Isolation: Art of Easter Island*, New York, The Metropolitan Museum of Art.

KOCH, GERD

1965   *Materielle Kulture der Santa Cruz-Inseln: Unter Besonderer Berüksichtigung der Riff-Inseln*, Berlin: Museum für Völkerkunde.

KOOIJMAN, SIMON

1972   *Tapa In Polynesia*, Bernice P. Bishop Museum Bulletin 234, Honolulu: Bishop Museum Press.

1988   *Polynesian Barkcloth*, Princess Risborough: Shire Publications, Ltd.

KUYKENDALL, RALPH S.

1980 [1938]   *The Hawaiian Kingdom: 1778-1874*, Honolulu: University Press of Hawaii.

LAMAR, CHRISTINE

1995   Unpublished manuscript, genealogical research into the identity of Daniel T. Aborn.

LAVONDÈS, ANNE

1995   "La Société Traditionnelle" in Michel Panoff, ed. Trésors des îles Marquises, Paris: Réunion des Musées Nationaux.

LEONARD, ANNE AND JOHN TERRELL

1980   *Patterns of Paradise, The Styles and Significance of Barkcloth Around the World*, Chicago: Field Museum of Natural History.

MACK, CHARLES

1982   Polynesian Art at Auction 1965-1980, Northboro: Mack-Nasser Publishing, Inc.

MARTIN, JOHN
1827   An Account of the Natives of the Tonga Islands in the South Pacific Ocean, with an Original Grammar and Vocabulary of their Language. Compiled and Arranged from the Extensive Communications of Mr. William Mariner, Several Years Resident of those Islands, Edinburg: Constable and Company; London: Hurst, Chance and Co.

MATSUOKA, SHIZUO
1927   Micronesia Minzoku Shi [Micronesian Folk Customs], Tokyo: Oka Shoin.

METRAUX, ALFRED
1971 [1940]   Ethnology of Easter Island, Honolulu: Bishop Museum Press.

NEICH, ROGER
2000   Personal interview with the author. October 4.

NEICH, ROGER AND MICK PENDERGRAST
1998 [1997]   Traditional Tapa Textiles of the Pacific, New York: Thames and Hudson.

OLDMAN, W. O.
The Oldman Collection of Polynesian Artifact. Memoirs of the Polynesian Society, vol. 15. New Plymouth.

PELRINE, DIANE M.
1996   Affinities of Form: Arts of Africa, Oceania, and the Americas from the Raymond and Laura Wielgus Collection, Munich and London: Prestel Verlag.

PHELPS, STEPHEN
1976   Art and Artefacts of the Pacific, Africa and the Americas: The James Hooper Collection, London: Hutchinson & Co. Limited.

PRITCHARD, MARY J.
1984   "Siapo: Bark Cloth of Samoa," Council on Culture, Arts and Humanities, Special Publication 1, American Samoa: Council on Culture, Arts and Humanities.

ROBLEY, HORATIO GORDON
1896   Moko; or Maori Tattooing, London: Chapman and Hall, Limited.

ROSE, ROGER C.
1980   Hawaii: The Royal Isles, Bernice P. Bishop Museum Special Publication 67, Honolulu: Bishop Museum Press.

SIMMONS, DAVID R.
"Te Rarangi Taonga, Catalogue" in Mead, Sidney Moko, ed. Te Maori, 176-235, New York: Harry N. Abrahms, Inc.

1989   Maori Tattoo: Ko Te Riria, Auckland: The Bush Press.

SMITH, PERCY S.
1910   Maori Wars of the Nineteenth Century: The Struggle of the Northern against the Southern Maori Tribes prior to the Colonisation (sic) of New Zealand in 1840, Christchurch, Wellington and Dunedin; Melbourne and London: Whitcombe & Tombs Limited.

SOMERVILLE, B.T.
1897   "Ethnographical Notes in New Georgia, Solomon Islands," Journal of the Royal Anthropological Institute 26: 357-412.

SOTHEBY PARKE BERNET & CO.
1978   Catalogue of the George Ortiz Collection of African and Oceanic Works of Art, London: Sotheby Parke Bernet & Co.

SOTHEBY'S
1986   Important Tribal Art, (auction catalogue, November 18), New York: Sotheby's.

ST. CARTMAIL, KEITH
1997   The Art of Tonga: "Ko E Ngaahi'Aati' O Tonga", Honolulu: University of Hawaii Press.

STARZECKA, DOROTA CZARKOWSKA
1975   Hawaii: People and Culture, London: Trustees of the British Museum.

STEINEN, KARL VON DEN
1969 [1928]   Die Marquesaner und ihre Kunst, vol. II, Die Plastik, Berlin: Reimer.

TREIDE, BARBARA
1997   In den Weiten des Pazifik Mikronseien, Wiesbaden: Dr. Ludwig Reichert Verlag.

WAITE, DEBORAH B.
1983   Art of the Solomon Islands from the Collection of the Barbier-Müller Museum. Geneva: Musée Barbier-Müller.

WARD, GERARD R., ED.
American Activities in the Central Pacific 1790-1870, Ridgewood: The Gregg Press.

WAVELL, BARBARA B.
1998   The Art of Micronesia, Maitland: The Maitland Art Center.

WILLIAMSON, ROBERT W.
1924   The Social and Political Systems of Central Polynesia, Cambridge: Cambridge University Press.

1939   Essays in Polynesian Ethnology, Piddington, Ralph, (ed.) Cambridge: Cambridge University Press.

WILKES, CHARLES
1970 [1845]   Narrative of the United States Exploring Expedition. During the Years 1838, 1839, 1840, 1841, 1842. Upper Saddle River: The Gregg Press.

WOODFORD, C.M.
1909   "The Canoes of the British Solomon Islands," Journal of the Royal Anthropological Institute XXXIX: 506-516, pl. XL-XLIV.

YATE, WILLIAM
1835   An Account of New Zealand and of the Formation and Progress of the Church Missionary Society's Mission in the Northern Island, London: Seeley and Burnside.